# Evil Plans

# EVIL
# PLANS

Having Fun on the Road
to World Domination

## Hugh MacLeod

PORTFOLIO / PENGUIN

PORTFOLIO / PENGUIN
Published by the Penguin Group
Penguin Group (USA) Inc., 375 Hudson Street, New York, New York 10014, U.S.A· • Penguin Group (Canada), 90 Eglinton Avenue East, Suite 700, Toronto, Ontario, Canada M4P 2Y3 (a division of Pearson Penguin Canada Inc.) • Penguin Books Ltd, 80 Strand, London WC2R ORL, England • Penguin Ireland, 25 St Stephen's Green, Dublin 2, Ireland (a division of Penguin Books Ltd) • Penguin Books Australia Ltd, 250 Camberwell Road, Camberwell, Victoria 3124, Australia (a division of Pearson Australia Group Pty Ltd) • Penguin Books India Pvt Ltd, 11 Community Centre, Panchsheel Park, New Delhi - 110 017, India • Penguin Group (NZ), 67 Apollo Drive, Rosedale, North Shore 0632, New Zealand (a division of Pearson New Zealand Ltd) • Penguin Books (South Africa) (Pty) Ltd, 24 Sturdee Avenue, Rosebank, Johannesburg 2196, South Africa

Penguin Books Ltd, Registered Offices:
80 Strand, London WC2R 0RL, England

First published in 2011 by Portfolio / Penguin,
a member of Penguin Group (USA) Inc.

10  9  8  7  6  5  4  3  2  1

Selections from this book first appeared on the author's website, gapingvoid.com.

Library of Congress Cataloging-in-Publication Data

MacLeod, Hugh, 1965-
Evil plans : having fun on the road to world domination / Hugh MacLeod.
p. cm.
ISBN 978-1-59184-384-9
1. Job satisfaction.  2. Quality of work life.  3. Entrepreneurship.  I. Title.
HF5549.5.J63M165 2011
650.1—dc22        2010039729

Printed in the United States of America
Designed by Daniel Lagin

*Evil Plans* is dedicated to my father, **WILLIAM MACLEOD** (1938–2010), who passed away the very same weekend I sent off the final manuscript of this book to my editor for publishing. People who knew Dad will see a lot of him in this book—he taught me very well. He is sorely missed.

# Contents

# CONTENTS

# Evil Plans

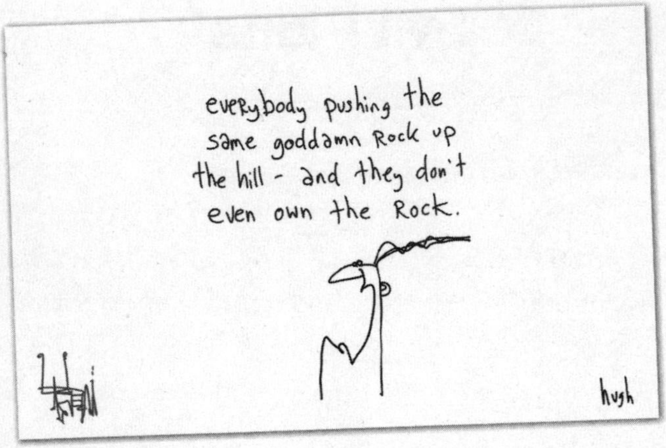
everybody pushing the same goddamn Rock up the hill - and they don't even own the Rock.
hugh

# Introduction: "Everybody Needs an Evil Plan"

**EVERYBODY NEEDS AN EVIL PLAN. EVERYBODY** needs that crazy, out-there idea that allows them to *actually* start doing something they love, doing something that matters. Everybody needs an Evil Plan that gets them the hell out of the rat race, away from lousy bosses, away from boring, dead-end jobs that they hate. Life is short.

Every person who ever managed to do this, every person who managed to escape the cubicle farm and start doing something interesting and meaningful, started off with their own Evil Plan. And yeah, pretty much everyone around them—friends, family, colleagues—thought they were nuts.

Thanks to the Internet, it has never been easier to have an Evil Plan, to make a great living, doing what you love, doing something that matters. My intention is that by the time you've finished reading this book, you will completely concur. More important, you'll actually feel compelled enough to go and do something about it yourself, if you haven't already.

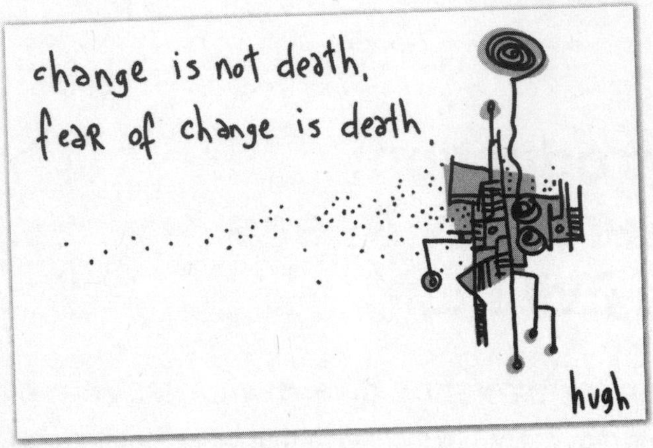
change is not death.
fear of change is death.
hugh

## "TO UNIFY WORK AND LOVE"

Sigmund Freud once said that in order to be truly happy in life, a human being needed to acquire two things: the capacity to work, and the capacity to love.

An Evil Plan is really about being able to do both at the same time.

At time of writing of this book, I've been blogging at gapingvoid.com for just shy of a decade. I've done a lot of stuff with it since I started. Published cartoons, sold wine, sold suits, plugged Microsoft, plugged Dell, sold art, "built my personal brand," written e-books, ranted on endlessly about marketing, new media, and all sorts . . .

But looking back, I realize it all served a common purpose: to unify work and love. I was writing about what was most interesting and important to me, and trying to turn it into a career somehow.

Then I noticed, the people who have inspired me the most these last couple of years—entrepreneurs, writers, artists— they were driven by the same thing: to get paid doing what they love. And they all found a way to make it happen, without exception.

Are you one of the people who can unify work and love? If not, don't you think you should be? I mean, after friends and family, what the hell is there?

it was either love what i do or hate what i do. i chose the former.

hugh

## WORLD DOMINATION

Everyone lives in their own little world. The planet is just too damn big for one person to take it all in. So every human being seeks out their own little microcosm. Whether we're talking about Wall Street, the coffee shops of bohemian Chicago, the ranches of West Texas or the San Francisco advertising agency scene, we find these worlds that suit us (sometimes they find us too), and we pitch our tents there.

These worlds are the ones we want to dominate. We all know where and what they are. . . .

You don't really aim to "dominate" the world you live in, of course. The most you can hope for is to live in harmony with it. You like it, it likes you back. Things just work. Things just click. And when your Evil Plan is going full steam, this is how it all feels.

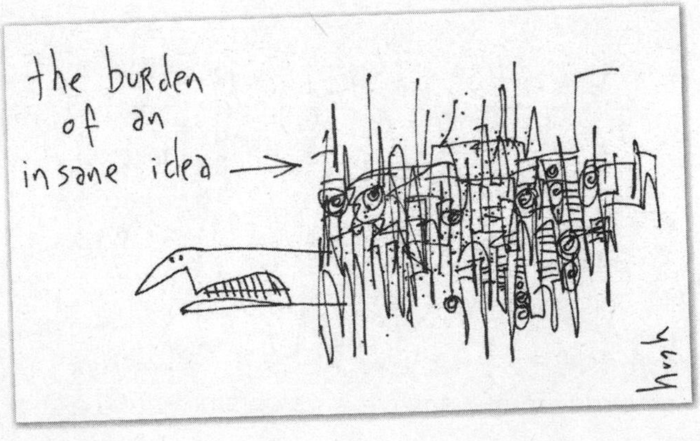
the burden of an insane idea
hugh

# THE GENESIS OF MY OWN EVIL PLAN

The first few years of this century were tough ones for me. My career in advertising pretty much tanked around the same time as the dotcom crash, and I found myself unemployed, broke, living in the boonies, scraping a meager freelance living by writing brochure copy. Then 9/11 came along, plunged everything into fear and chaos, and made everything even worse. Not fun or nice.

Up until that point, I had spent my entire working career "chasing gigs." Whether we're talking full-time salaried positions or three-day freelance opportunities, I had spent well over a decade chasing that ever-elusive island of security in a swelling ocean of advertising-industry chaos. And these gigs would never last; they would always end eventually, for whatever reason. Recessions, layoffs, downsizing, incompetence on my part, incompetence on the boss's part—whatever. And usually the timing was bad.

Chase, chase, chase . . . And I was sick of it. Really, *really* sick of it. More than a decade of working my butt off, and those islands of security were no less elusive than before. And I wasn't as young as I used to be. The hamster wheel was starting to do me in.

Then, in these darkest of days, I had a sudden flash of life-changing insight. Like I told my fellow advertising-burnout drinking buddy that evening, as we commiserated at the bar about our sad lot in life, "I don't want to be 'chasing gigs' any-more."

"What do you want, then?" asked my buddy.

"I just want ten thousand people giving me money every year."

"Where are you going to find these people?" he asked.

"The Internet," I replied.

"What do you plan on doing there?"

"I think I'll start by publishing my cartoons online ... on a blog."

"What's a 'blog'? ... "

So that was my Evil Plan. To get ten thousand people a year to buy my stuff, via the Internet. I succeeded eventually, and then some. Happy ending.

What? Make a good living, doing what you love, without being accountable to some larger company, organization or secret cabal of "A-listers"? You're not supposed to do that, MacLeod, you're supposed to clock in every morning after a lousy commute, just like the rest of us. You're supposed to hate your job, just like the rest of us. You're supposed to be stressed out and beholden to the system, just like the rest of us.

It's funny, but all these years later, and it still bugs some people that I managed to pull it off. No wonder I had jokingly called my plan "evil." According to these guys, I must somehow be doing something morally reprehensible, to not be playing by their usual, unspoken rules of the relentlessly oppressive status quo, not living in the proverbial "quiet desperation."

And of course, this social resistance will come to you, too, if you try to follow your own Evil Plan. It's not that people don't want you to be successful—they just don't want you to be successful in ways they aspire to be but cannot be themselves. That is just human nature, sad but true.

To hell with it. Finding and implementing your own Evil Plan is without question one of the greatest things you can do with the brief time you're allotted on this earth. And along the way, just like me, you'll meet some incredible, like-minded people, determined to do the same: make a good living doing what they love, doing something that matters, becoming the person they were born to be despite the odds. Finding that. Doing that. Discovering "the Hunger" that lives inside all of us.

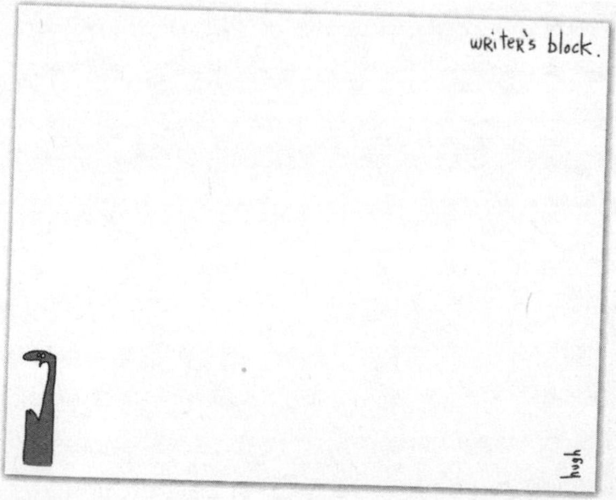
writer's block.
hugh

as long as
you feel
inspiRed
your life
is being
well spent.

hugh

# Welcome to the Hunger

## IT WILL COST YOU YOUR LIFE.

*The Hunger to do something creative.*

*The Hunger to do something amazing.*

*The Hunger to change the world.*

*The Hunger to make a difference.*

*The Hunger to enjoy one's work.*

*The Hunger to be able to look back and say, Yeah, cool,
   I did that.*

*The Hunger to make the most of this utterly brief blip of time
   Creation has given us.*

*The Hunger to dream the good dreams.*

*The Hunger to have amazing people in our lives.*

*The Hunger to have the synapses continually firing on
   overdrive.*

*The Hunger to experience beauty.*

*The Hunger to tell the truth.*

*The Hunger to be part of something bigger than yourself.*

*The Hunger to have good stories to tell.*

*The Hunger to stay the course, despite the odds.*

*The Hunger to feel passion.*

*The Hunger to know and express Love.*

*The Hunger to know and express Joy.*

*The Hunger to channel the Divine.*

*The Hunger to actually feel alive.*

The Hunger will give you everything. And it will take from you, everything. It will cost you your life, and there's not a damn thing you can do about it.

But knowing this, of course, is what ultimately sets you free.

My name is
hugh macleod.
and Right now
i'm cRying.

hugh

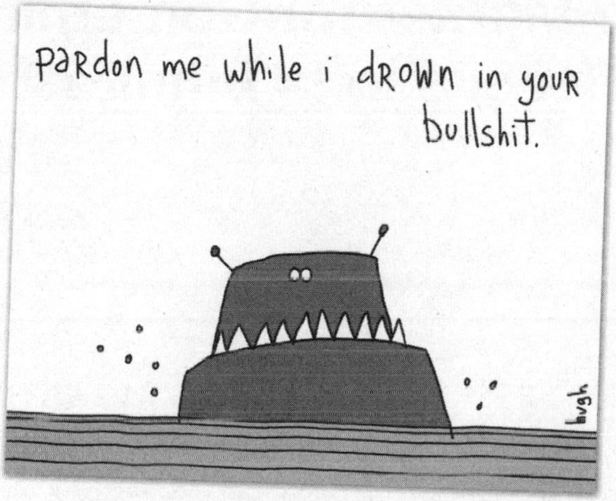
pardon me while i drown in your bullshit.
hugh

# The Market for Something to Believe In Is Infinite

"We are here to find meaning. We are here to help other people do the same. Everything else is secondary."

**NEAR THE TAIL END OF MY ADVERTISING** career, circa 2004, I wrote a little rant on my blog that was eventually christened "The Hughtrain Manifesto." It encapsulated everything important I knew about marketing, up to that point. I've copied the latest edit below:

> **THE HUGHTRAIN MANIFESTO: "THE MARKET FOR SOMETHING TO BELIEVE IN IS INFINITE."**
>
> We are here to find meaning. We are here to help other people do the same. Everything else is secondary.
> We humans want to believe in our own species. And we

want people, companies, and products in our lives that make it easier for us to believe in one another. That is human nature.

Product benefit doesn't excite us. Belief in humanity and human potential excites us.

Think less about what your product does, and think more about human potential. What statement about humanity does your product make?

The bigger the statement, the bigger the idea, the bigger your brand will become.

It's no longer enough for people to believe that your product does what it says on the label. They want to believe in you and what you do. And they'll go elsewhere if they don't.

It's not enough for the customer to love your product. They have to love your process as well.

People are not getting more demanding just as consumers, they are getting more demanding as spiritual entities. Branding becomes a spiritual exercise.

Either get with the program or hire a consultant in Extinction Management. No vision, no business. Your life from now on pivots squarely on your vision of human potential.

The primary job of an advertiser is not to communicate benefit but to communicate conviction.

Benefit is secondary. Benefit is a product of conviction, not vice versa.

Whatever you manufacture, somebody can make it better, faster, and cheaper than you.

You do not own the molecules. They are stardust. They belong to God. What you do own is your soul. Nobody can take that away from you. And it is your soul that informs the brand.

It is your soul, and the purpose and beliefs your soul embodies, that people will buy into.

Why is your Evil Plan great? Why does your Evil Plan matter? Seriously. If you don't know, then nobody else can—no advertiser, no buyer, and certainly no customer.

It's not about merit. It's about faith. Belief. Conviction. Courage.

It's about why you're on this planet. To "make a dent in the universe."

I don't want to know why your product is good or very good or even great. I want to know why *you* are totally frickin' amazing.

Once you tell me, I can tell the world.

And then they will know.

Here's the point: Whatever you're selling isn't merely a product or service, it's also a product of a belief system—your own belief system. And understanding your belief system is crucial to building your own Evil Plan.

As my friend and mentor, the great marketing thinker Seth Godin, once said to me, "You can't drink any more bottled water than you already do. Or buy more wine. Or more tea. You can't wear more than one pair of shoes at a time. You can't get two massages at once. . . .

"So, what grows? What do marketers sell that scales?

"I'll tell you what: Belief. Belonging. Mattering. Making a difference. Tribes. We have an unlimited need for this."

Another friend of mine, the film director David Mackenzie once quipped, "A film is only as good as the reasons for making it."

What is true for Hollywood is also true for products and businesses. It's not what you make, it's what you believe in. That is what people respond to. That is where your enterprise lives or dies.

So. Go believe in something. It really works. Trust me.

inspire.
be inspired.
hugh

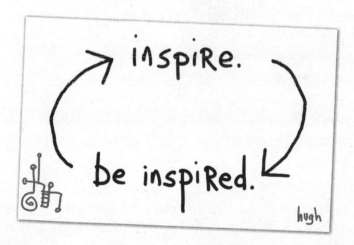

i don't need
RELIGION.
i've got an
iphone.

hugh

# Create Your Own Global Microbrand

In the Internet era, if people on the other side of
the planet aren't loving what you do, you're doing
something wrong.

**EVER SINCE I FIRST COINED THE TERM, I HAVE**
been totally besotted with the idea of "The Global Microbrand."

A small, tiny brand that "sells" all over the world.

Global microbrands are nothing new; they've existed for a
while—long before the Internet was invented. Imagine a well-
known author or painter selling his work all over the world. Or
a small whisky distillery in Scotland that exports to the United
States. Or a small cheese maker in rural France, whose product is exported to Paris, London, and beyond. Ditto with a violin
maker in Italy. A maker of classical guitars in Spain. A micro-
brewery in Washington that exports its beers to twenty-four
other states. Or a small British firm that makes $50,000 shot-
guns for collectors and enthusiasts the world over.

With the Internet, of course, a global microbrand is easier to create than ever before. A commercial sign maker in New England or a small sheet-metal entrepreneur in the U.K. can use the Internet, blogs, social media, and whatnot to spread the word, to talk to people from all over.

Especially with the advent of blogs in the early years of this century, global microbranding no longer had to be limited to people who made products. We saw that any service professional with a bit of talent and something to say could spread their message far and wide beyond their immediate client base and local market, without needing a high-profile name or the goodwill of the mainstream media. Lawyers, IT consultants, marketing folk—you name it.

And global microbranding is not just limited to cottage industries, either. In the 1990s, the great business guru Tom Peters talked about "Brand You"—a personal brand that transcends your organization or job description. The godfather of this space is probably Robert Scoble, who worked full-time for Microsoft but via his high-traffic blog, his personal brand became much, much larger than any job description they could give him; and it was worth far more than anything they ever paid him.

Once I created my own fledgling global microbrand (via my blog), I started helping other people do the same. A bespoke English tailor. A small winery in South Africa. It was something I really wanted to know about. It was the most compelling idea I had ever come across in my professional career. I was hooked.

Of course, the global microbrand is not conceptual rocket

science. You don't need a Nobel Prize in order to understand the idea. What excites me about it is the fact that I now live in a small adobe in the far West Texas desert, and career-wise I'm getting a lot more done than when I lived in a large apartment in New York or London, and for a fifth of the overhead. With one-fiftieth of the stress levels. My job allows me to travel a lot—New York, Miami, San Francisco, São Paulo, etc. After three or four days away in the big city I start feeling really stressed out and ready to return to my adobe. For years I thought it was just me. But in fact *everyone* in the big city seems really stressed out. It's just considered normal.

I was recently talking to a friend on the phone about this.

"There's only two ways to deal with life in the big city," he said. "Alcohol and high prices. Immersing yourself in high-rent luxury items; trendy, overpriced cocktail bars; flashy restaurants; tall leggy blondes who don't give a damn about you . . . just to act as a buffer zone between you and the abyss."

"Which you pay a lot for," I said.

"Which you pay a hell of a lot for," he said.

It seems to me a lot of people of my generation are stuck on this high-priced, corporate, urban treadmill. Sure, they get paid a lot, but their overhead is also off the scale. The minute they stop tap-dancing as fast as they can is the minute they are crushed under the wheels of commerce. You know what? It's not sustainable.

However, the global microbrand *is* sustainable. With it you are not beholden to one boss, one company, one customer, one local economy, or even one industry. Your brand develops relationships in enough different places to the extent that your permanent address becomes almost irrelevant.

Frankly, it beats the hell out of commuting every morning to the corporate glass box in the big city—something I did for many years. Just so I could make enough money to help me forget that I have to commute every morning to the corporate glass box in the big city.

An ordinary job in a big company or a famous institution simply doesn't have the job security, social status, or personal satisfaction that it did even a generation ago. Which is why so many of us, in this era of the Internet and personal media, are looking for our own personal global microbrand. That is the prize. That is the way to get off the treadmill. And I don't think that's a bad "Evil Plan" to have.

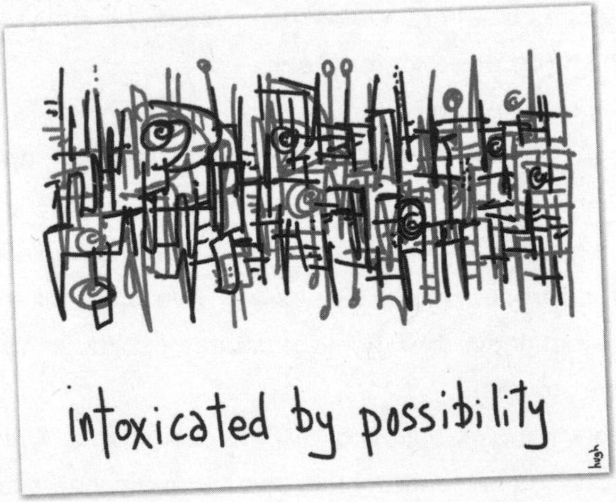
intoxicated by possibility
hugh

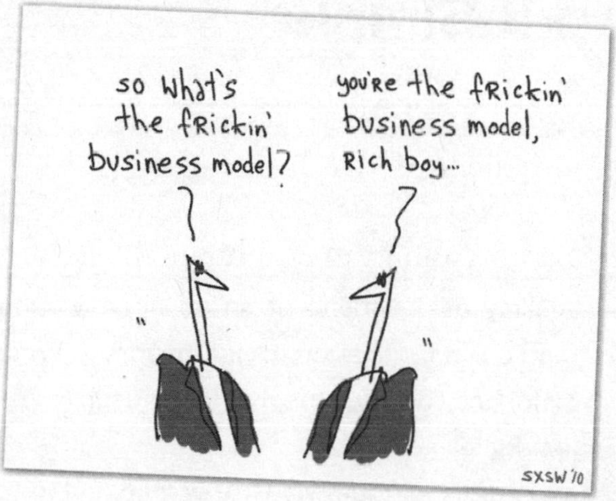
so what's the frickin' business model?
you're the frickin' business model, rich boy...
SXSW '10

# Keep It Simple

Avoid "complicated" like the plague.

**IN THE LATE 1990s I WAS LIVING IN NEW YORK** City, busting my ass, working at an ad agency. One day I decided to go down to Houston to visit my family. While I was there, my sister and I decided to drive up to Austin to visit some old college buddies.

Instead of our usual route via I-10, we decided to take the slower but more scenic Route 290, through the Texas Hill Country. A lovely drive of about 150 miles.

At about the halfway point we pull into Chappell Hill, Texas, a sweet little hamlet of maybe three hundred people. We stop for some gas.

Right next to the gas station is this small storefront, called the Chappell Hill Meat Market & Café. A traditional lunch diner taking up most of the building, and to the right, a tiny grocery store.

Turns out this hole-in-the wall grocery store sells some of the best Texas sausage and jerky you ever did come across. They have their own smokehouse in the back, and everything is prepared right there on the premises. My friends in Austin are having a barbecue that evening, so we buy about forty dollars' worth of sausage and jerky for the party. We eat some of the jerky in the car—outstanding!

We have a great time in Austin seeing our friends. Everybody *loved* the meat we brought for them. On our way home to Houston, because my sister and I liked the Chappell Hill Meat Market so much, we decide to stop in again and buy some more sausage for my dad and his wife.

As I'm paying for the food I compliment the person serving me, the owner, a nice lady named Cissy.

"This is a great little place," I say. "I *love* your meats."

"Why, thank you," says Cissy in her very polite Texan way.

"I bet you sell a lot of this stuff," I say.

"Sure do," says Cissy. "About a thousand pounds of meat..."

"A week? Really? That much?"

"No, darlin'. A thousand pounds every day."

*Boom!* A moment of clarity. A tiny little hole-in-the wall in Nowheresville, Texas. Selling three and a half *tons* of world-class product a week. Doing the math in my head, assuming they've got a reasonable margin, that's a lot more money than me or any of my other New York cronies were making (or probably ever going to make). For a lot less hassle and overhead, to boot.

Now, I never wanted to go into the meat business, but since that day in Central Texas, I have aspired to have a business model as simple, elegant, profitable, and low-key as this one. Every day, I'm getting closer.

And this, of course, is what *Evil Plans* is really all about. . . .

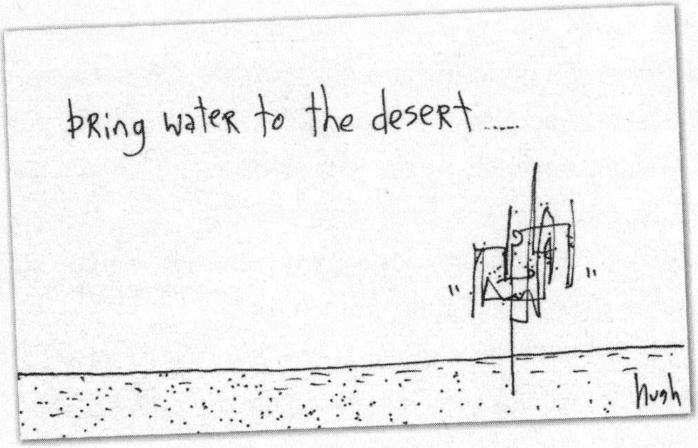
bring water to the desert....
hugh

here's a gun.
the minute i
become a slave
again, please use
it to shoot me.
hugh

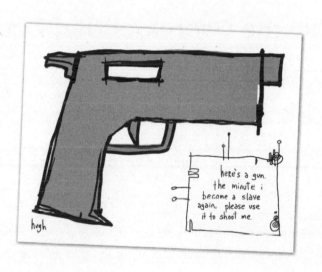

# Join the Overextended Class

"If ever there was a time to be overextended,
this is it."

—CHRIS ANDERSON, EDITOR IN CHIEF, *WIRED*

**BACK IN AUGUST 2009 I INTERVIEWED CHRIS**
Anderson, who at the time was editor in chief of one of my
favorite magazines, *Wired*:

> **Hugh:** You've got your Editor job, you've got your book deals,
> you've got your blog, you do a lot of speaking gigs . . . As your
> name gets more and more known, are you having trouble
> keeping up with everything? What's your coping mechanism?
> How do you find the balance?
>
> **Chris:** Plus the five little kids, the two start-up companies on
> the side, et cetera. Obviously, balance is a distant goal. In

the meantime, I delegate; work all the time; hardly sleep; totally ignore politics, sports, and pop culture; neglect my family too much; and probably don't do any of my jobs as well as I could. But these are exciting days, and if ever there was a time to be overextended, this is it.

I agree with him completely. I know what it means to be overextended all too well. Recently I made a list of all the projects I'm currently working on. My next writing project. The online fine-art print business I own (gapingvoidgallery.com). My budding little wine business. Blogging. Consulting. Drawing cartoons. The list goes on. . . .

All in all, it came down to ten items. Ten. Each one interesting and potentially lucrative enough to be taken on as a full-time job. Ten.

Ouch. Even for me, that seemed like *way* too much.

The other day, a friend of mine was kvetching about having to hold down two jobs. "Two?" I quipped. "Try holding down ten. . . ."

My friend looked at me funny. He was probably right to do so. The world he lives in was never designed to be as swamped as mine.

But since about 1991, it's been like that for me. From the moment I woke up till the moment I went to bed, I was working on something. The day job or the cartoons or something else. Sure, I'd have girlfriends come and go, but the girlfriends never lasted too long, and I also ended up inventing, in 1997, an art form that would allow me to carry on working *when* I was going out to the bars—i.e., the "Cartoons Drawn on the Back of Business Cards."

I've not had a proper vacation in ten years either. Nor am I planning one.

You can call Chris and me, and probably more than 50 percent of the people who are reading this book, members of "the overextended class."

You know who you are. And you know what? In terms of percentage of the population, there were fewer of us twenty years ago. And there'll be a lot more of us in two decades. That's just how the world of work is evolving.

It seems almost unbelievable now, but our parents and grandparents spent *huge* amounts of their free, "nonwork" time watching television. Passive, non-interactive media consumption will soon be mostly a thing of the past . . . a historical accident of the old factory-worker age meeting the modern mass-media age. Of course it wouldn't last forever. We humans as a species were designed to compete, not to sit around on our asses. We're designed to create, not to consume.

Welcome to the overextended class. You may opt out of it if you want, but over time it's going to get harder and harder to make ends meet, let alone be successful, if you do.

Decide.

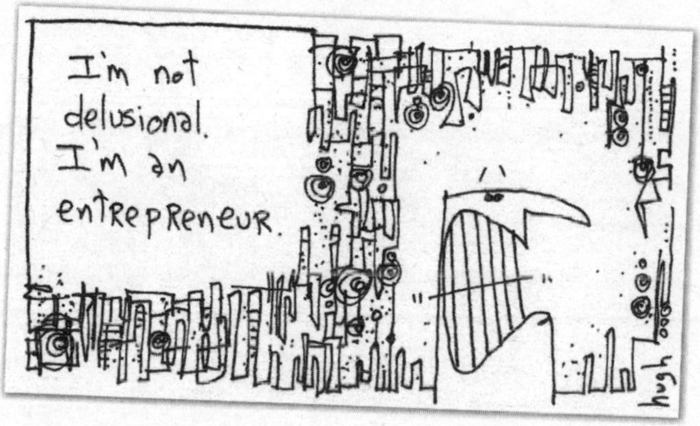
I'm not delusional. I'm an entrepreneur.
hugh

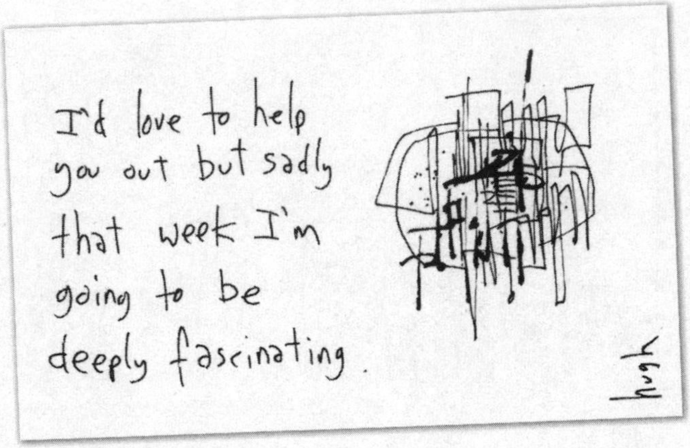
I'd love to help you out but sadly that week I'm going to be deeply fascinating.
hugh

# Have a World-Class Product

Mediocrity has had its day. That day is so over.

## THE CURIOUS STORY OF AN ENGLISH SAVILE ROW TAILOR AND AN UNDER-EMPLOYED CARTOONIST

In late 2004, things were still rough for me. I was still broke, underemployed, and wondering what the hell I was going to do next. The answer came from a direction I would never have expected.

At the time, I was living in Cumbria, in a cottage in the northern England boondocks, not far from the famous Lake District. I was just lying low, scraping a living doing freelance, trying to save money. It was a bleak and miserable time, frankly.

In the local village pub, I got friendly with a local fellow named Thomas Mahon. We were about the same age, and his business wasn't doing very well either.

Thomas was a tailor. He made suits. And not just any kind of suits. He made the best of the best—$5,000, handmade suits. He'd been trained on Savile Row, in London—the legendary British home of tailoring. Some say they make the best suits in the world there. He had made suits for rock stars, royalty, famous designers . . . you name it. He really was that good. The man who trained him, Dennis Halberry, was head cutter for Anderson & Sheppard, one of the most esteemed tailoring firms in the world.

A few years previously, Thomas had grown sick of working on Savile Row for Anderson & Sheppard, decided he missed his beloved Cumbria, and decided to move back home to set up shop in the village he grew up in, the same village we were having our beers.

Everyone told him he was mad to "Go off the Row," but he paid no attention. He was tired of London, he was homesick; he really didn't care.

Though he was one of the most respected young tailors on Savile Row, it turns out he wasn't very good at getting the word out about his work. His customers loved him, but they didn't like to tell other people about him. They wanted him all to themselves. So in spite of his formidable talent, Thomas wasn't getting one-fifth the business he deserved.

So there we were, Christmas approaching, and in spite of us both feeling a bit gloomy about our current economic situation, we were cheerily sitting in the local pub one evening, with Thomas telling me all of these wonderful stories about the people and experiences of working on Savile Row.

Finally I interrupted him.

"Tom," I said, "these Savile Row stories are terrific. You should blog about them."

"What's a blog?" he asked.

By this time I had been blogging for about three years and knew all about how it worked. That night, we came up with an Evil Plan. I would show Tom how to blog, he would make the suits, I would figure out a way to spread the word online.

EnglishCut.com was born.

Instead of using the blog to hard-sell his suits, Thomas just wrote these great little blog posts about the world he knew and loved—the community of Savile Row tailors. He'd write about it all—his friends on the Row, the pubs they drank in, the other businesses on the Row. He just wrote about it honestly, with great passion and affection. He even praised the other shops, his competition. Why not? They were all good people, with second-to-none skills.

A few years later, Thomas would confide in me that he never thought anyone would ever find what he wrote about to be that interesting. So, not expecting anybody to read it, he just wrote it his way. If he had thought a lot of people would be interested in it, he would have written it differently. More uptight. Less transparent.

And boy, was he wrong about his audience in the end. People *loved* his blog. They *adored* the transparency and Thomas's easygoing, unpretentious manner. So much so that within no time at all, he had gone from underemployed tailor to having a two-year waiting list, just to get a first appointment.

If you go online and Google "Thomas Mahon" or "English Cut," you'll find a lot to read about. The story got a lot of attention in the blogopsphere back then, simply because in 2005, an English Savile Row tailor was probably the person you'd least expect to start a blog. But it worked. And it worked *amazingly* well.

Thomas and I worked together for a few more years before amicably going our separate ways. It was one of the most rewarding career moves I ever made. And I think Thomas would say the same.

My father once remarked to me, "I bet you had no idea in the beginning that the blog would work as well as it did, eh?"

True, I had no idea. But looking back, we had a few things going for us:

1. **A great product.** Thomas is one of the best tailors in the world. His suits *really are* that good. If we were just selling commodified dreck, I doubt anyone would've paid much attention.
2. **A unique story.** When he started, Thomas was the only Savile Row tailor writing a blog, and this gave him a unique voice in the blogosphere. This fueled the interest. Had

masses of tailors already been blogging, it would've been much harder for his own unique "meme" to spread. The first-mover-advantage rule still applies.

3. **Passion and authority.** Thomas has both in spades. That's what kept people coming back. That's what built up trust. That's what turned his readers into customers. Which is why "Share what you love" is the best advice there is.

4. **Continuity.** He kept at it. He didn't expect the blog to transform his fortunes overnight. As I'm fond of saying, "Blogs don't write themselves." Based on our experience, if you want a blog to transform your business, I'd say give yourself at least a year.

5. **Focus.** It was always about the suits. It was never about what he had for breakfast, Google traffic, or frothy gossip about other bloggers.

6. **Thomas spoke in his own voice.** Thomas is a straightforward, affable fellow, and the voice on the blog is the same as the voice you'd meet in real life. He never tried to misrepresent himself on his blog, nor did he try to create some over-glamorized image of his profession. He just told it like it is. And people responded well to that. As he once put it, "We're so lucky we don't have to create the brand out of thin air. We just tell the truth and the brand builds itself."

7. **Sovereignty.** The only people we had to please were the two of us. No bosses or outside investors to keep happy. Bosses and investors like to have guarantees, but there aren't any.

8. **We were both broke when we started.** If we'd had large sums of money at the beginning, we would have had a lot more options on how to get the word out, how to scale the business. In all likelihood, these options would have been a lot more expensive and not nearly as effective. Sometimes lack of capital is a definite advantage.

A blog is a great way to build one's own personal "global microbrand." Since the "job for life" no longer exists, and as the social value of the "position" erodes and the value of the "project" takes its place, personal brand development becomes far more important to one's career. Blogs are a good place to start. Is a blog an essential part of an Evil Plan? No. But it certainly worked well for Thomas and countless others I know personally.

Hey, if an old-school, technophobic Savile Row tailor can do it, what's your excuse?

all good ideas must die
(so that great ideas might live)
hugh

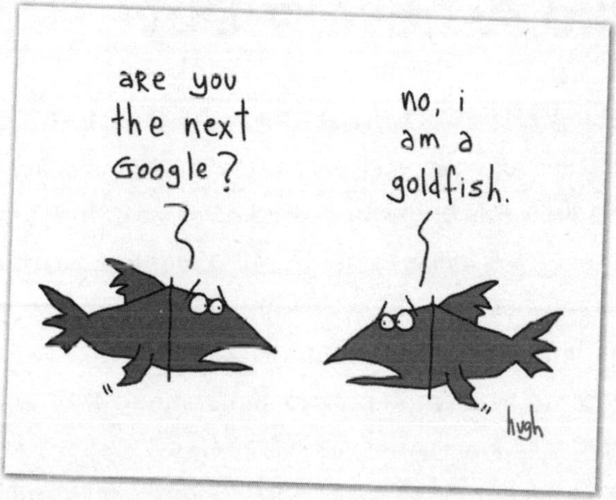
are you the next Google?
no, i am a goldfish.
hugh

# Make Art Every Day

**I MEET YOUNG, CREATIVE PEOPLE ALL THE** time, just out of college. They're tending bar, waiting tables, stacking shelves in bookstores, folding jeans at the Gap, working in offices. All trying to get by, all trying to figure out what to do next, where they fit in this big ol' world of ours. And it's tough for most of them. Of course it is.

My advice to them is always the same: "Make Art Every Day."

When I tell people to make "art," I don't necessarily mean paintings or literature or music or what-have-you. By "art" I mean whatever it is that's most meaningful and powerful to them.

Only they can know what that is, of course. My art was always drawing cartoons. But for others, it could be about business or cooking or carpentry or screen-printing T-shirts or raising money for charity. Like Ella Fitzgerald used to sing, "T'aint What You Do (It's the Way That You Do It)."

That was my Evil Plan for years. I remember being in my

mid-twenties, working all day long at the ad agency in Chicago. Then after work, instead of going home to watch TV and hang out with roommates or whatever, I'd head for my local coffee shop, pull a stool up at the bar, and sit there for hours on end, drawing cartoons. I would just keep drawing. Even if my cartoons weren't very good, even if they weren't commercial. Even if some of the waiters and fellow customers would make the occasional quip about me "needing to get a life."

It paid off eventually. Eventually the cartoons got good, eventually they got commercial. Eventually I didn't need a day job anymore, eventually I got a life. Happy ending.

I didn't wait for the money, I didn't wait to "be discovered," I didn't wait for the approval from others. I just got on with it, every day.

Like a very talented pianist once told me when I was a boy, it's better to practice a musical instrument for five minutes a day than to practice for two hours once a week. It's something I never forgot.

Which is why regardless of what the rest of the world needed from me on any given day, I found the time, somehow. Simply because I made the decision to do so, somehow.

Whatever your Evil Plan might be, "Make Art Every Day."

Why is "creativity"
such a dirty word
for big companies?
because it's something
that requires you
to put your balls
on the line.

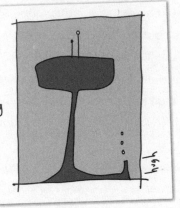

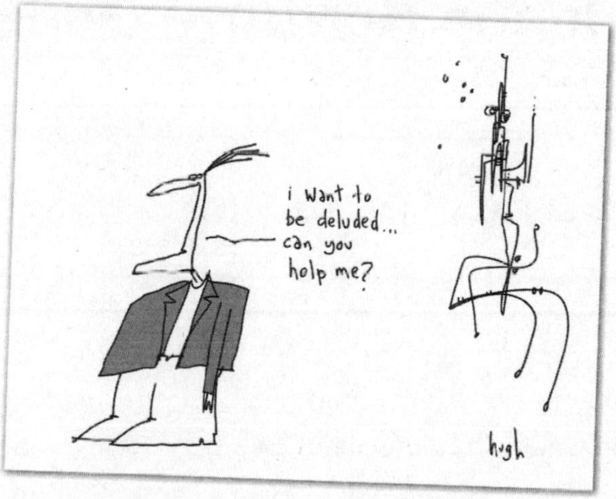
i want to be deluded... can you help me?
hugh

# Fill In the Narrative Gaps

Have a story. And make sure it's a good one. A *damn* good one.

**I HAVE A VERY OLD DEAR FRIEND IN NEW** York—let's call him Andrew.

Andrew is about forty, and he's a pretty successful film director. One of his films aired on HBO recently. He's been nominated for an Emmy before. He also has a thriving corpo-rate video business, which he works on when business in Hol-lywood is going slow any given month. He's not a household name, but he's done very well.

When I first met Andrew he was in his late twenties, working as a Manhattan bartender. Back then he had a vague idea of getting into the film business someday, but I didn't know how serious he was, to be honest. A lot of twentysomethings in New York blather on about getting into film; one tends to mostly ignore it.

But how Andrew eventually broke into the film business is one of my favorite tales.

In the late 1990s Andrew finally decides that he's serious about breaking into the industry. So he goes out and buys himself a small video camera, a sound recorder, a new Macintosh computer to do his editing, a few lights, some microphones . . . that kind of thing.

So the good news is, he now has all the gear he needs to get started.

The bad news is, having spent all his savings to acquire the gear, suddenly he needs money in a hurry. New York is expensive, and he's broke.

But because he had pretty much zero experience in the film business at that point, he soon realizes that it'll be a while before anyone in the traditional New York film industry will hire him for the kind of money he's looking for.

He can't afford to wait that long. So how does he pay the rent?

He decides to go into porn.

But not just any kind of porn. He does *personalized* porn.

Let's say you and your significant other want to create, shall we say, a special memento [*cough*] of your love [*cough*], and want something a bit more upmarket [*cough*] than just the normal, amateur, single-angle, unedited video from a camera [*cough*] that's standing on a tripod near the bed.

That's right. You'd give Andrew a call. And Andrew and his sound man would come over to your apartment and shoot you and your significant other [*cough*] going at it. With proper edits, lighting, sound, and camera angles. You and your loved one in the throes of passion [*cough*], with Andrew and the sound man hovering around you in silence, getting the perfect shot.

After he had shot the video, he would then take out his computer and edit the job right then and there, on the kitchen table. So before he left your home, he'd have already given you the *single* and *only* copy that existed of the video. He and his sound man would then exit with nothing—that is, with no backup copy on his computer, so there was no chance of the footage ending up on the Internet. At least, not from Andrew's side.

He charged a few hundred bucks for his services. The average shoot only took an hour or two. He would often do more than one shoot a day. On a good day, he could clear a thousand dollars. Damn good money for an ex-bartender. A lot more money than I ever made in New York.

Business was brisk from day one, as you might imagine. When he first told me what he'd been up to, back around 2000, I liked the story so much, I pitched the idea to a journalist friend of mine. Andrew ended up being featured in a fairly high-end magazine soon afterward, which raised his profile even more. Within no time, the phone was ringing off the hook with all sorts of interesting people—both inside and outside the film industry—wanting to do business with him.

Great story. There's only one catch.

I was talking to Andrew on the phone recently, catching up with my old buddy. I asked him if he would mind me using his "personalized porn" story for a possible chapter in *"Evil Plans"* as a case study for interesting and original business models.

"Sure, Hugh, go right ahead," he said. "Just one thing. None of it is true."

"Huh?"

"I made the whole thing up."

"What?" I said. "My favorite story about you ever, the one I've been telling folks with glee for the last ten years, was a total lie?!"

"Yes."

"Man, you're a good liar," I said.

"You knew that about me already," he said.

"Wow."

"Look," he said, "back then I was just one of thousands of young wannabe film knuckleheads in New York, trying to get my foot in the door. I needed to have a story to tell people. One that was interesting. One that was different. One that got people's attention. One that made me stand out from all the other knuckleheads. One that didn't require me having a massive show reel. And hey, it worked. That story got me my first few editing jobs in the business. And since then I've been nothing but successful."

He paused for a second.

"A little present-tense success forgives a lot of past-tense bullshitting," he said, chuckling with delight.

Now, I wouldn't recommend for a second that you follow Andrew's example and make your story up. Living in permanent fear of being found out is no way to live. Truth trumps fiction, every time.

But Andrew was right about one thing: *Human beings need to tell stories.* Historically, it's the quickest way we have for transmitting useful information to other members of our species. Stories are not simply nice things to have; they are essential survival tools.

And yes, the stories we tell ourselves are just as important as the stories we tell other people.

And yes, Andrew had the ability to fill in the narrative gaps.

Ergo, your Evil Plan is not about selling per se. It's more about figuring out where your product stands in relation to personal narrative. If people like buying your product, it's because its story helps fill in the narrative gaps in their own lives.

So where does your product or service or art fit into other people's narrative? How does telling your story become a survival tool for other people? If you don't know, you have a marketing—ahem, *storytelling*—problem.

Narrative gaps. It's all about the narrative gaps.

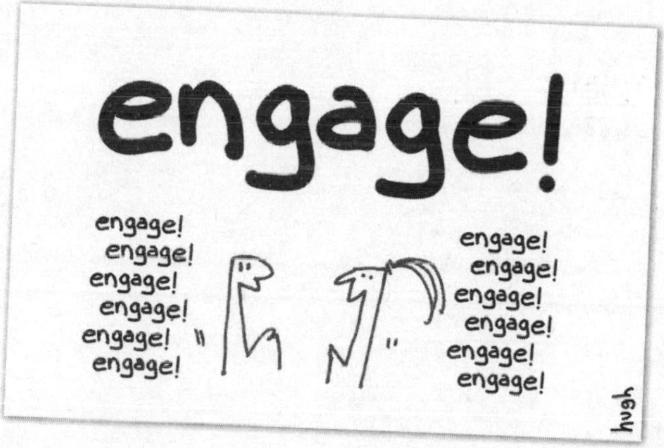
engage!
engage!
engage!
engage!
engage!
engage!
engage!
engage!
engage!
engage!
engage!
engage!
engage!
hugh

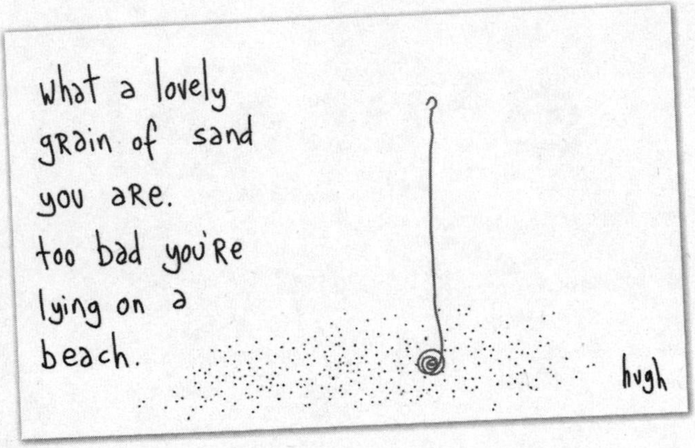
what a lovely grain of sand you are. too bad you're lying on a beach.
hugh

# Remember Who You Really Are

Remember that *Evil Plans* isn't just about making money. It's about becoming the person you need to be. If money's part of that, fine. If it isn't, that's fine too.

**THERE'S A WONDERFUL METAPHOR IN THE** Bible [Revelation 2:17] about a "white pebble."

> Let the one who has an ear hear what the spirit says to the congregations: To him that conquers I will give some of the hidden manna, and I will give him a white pebble, and upon the pebble a new name written which no one knows except the one receiving it.

The metaphor was once explained to me by a monk. To paraphrase—"you have three selves: the person you think you are, the person other people think you are, and the person God thinks you are. The white pebble represents the third one. And of the three, it is by far the most important."

He then gave me some good advice, something I've always kept with me:

"When life gets really tough, just remember the white pebble. Just remember who you *really* are. Just remember the person that *only God* can see."

Whatever your thoughts on God or religion may be, positive or negative, the white pebble is a very simple and strong metaphor that audaciously asks the question "Who are you, really?"

Yes, why are you here, exactly? *Who are you here for?* Yourself? Other people? Family? God? Money? Power? Fun? Sex and drugs? Fame? Science? Art? Or maybe some other cause? You tell me. . . .

It's one of those questions that never gets old. Unlike the poor body that houses us.

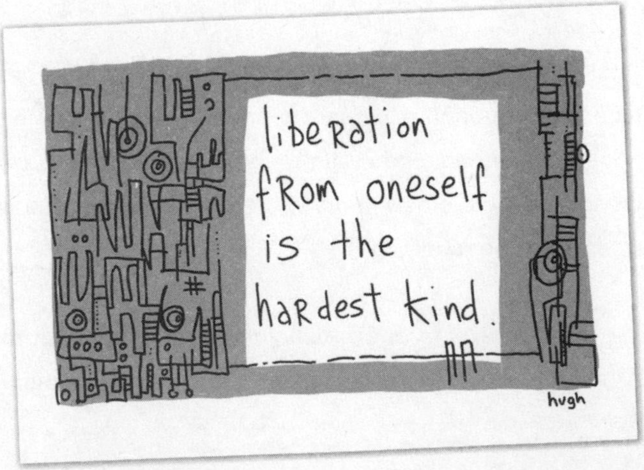
liberation from oneself is the hardest kind.
hugh

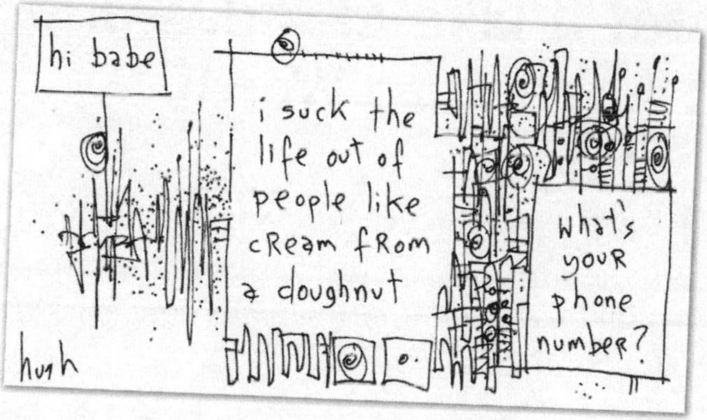
hi babe
i suck the life out of people like cream from a doughnut
what's your phone number?
hugh

# Treat It Like an Adventure— an Adventure Worth Sharing

If you can't get excited about your new Evil Plan, why should anyone else?

**I RECENTLY BOUGHT THE URL FUTILEMARKETING.COM.**

No, I'm not planning on turning it into another website, nor am I planning to launch a new business called "Futile Marketing." It's just a name I very much wanted to own.

Why? Because "futility" as a marketing strategy is an idea that's fascinating to me.

Conventional wisdom dictates that if you're trying to market something, the last thing you want your marketing campaign to be is *"An Act of Futility."*

But . . . are you *really* sure about that?

I was thinking recently how many great ideas started out as acts of futility:

- Getting people to pay $4 for a cup of coffee started off as an act of futility—Starbucks.
- Getting people to give up their horses en masse in exchange for an internal combustion engine started off as an act of futility—Ford Motors.
- Getting people to pay for software without any hardware attached to it started off as an act of futility—Microsoft.
- Turning a one-man tech blog into a multimillion-dollar online news service using nothing but blog advertising started off as an act of futility—TechCrunch.com.
- Writing a children's book about wizards in an Edinburgh coffee shop and then finding somebody who wanted to publish it started off as an act of futility—*Harry Potter.*
- Trying to halt the Nazi invasion using nothing but a small number of Spitfires and Hurricanes started off as an act of futility—the Battle of Britain.
- Stopping the largest army the world had ever seen with just a small phalanx of 300 Spartans started off as an act of futility—the Battle of Thermopylae.
- Trying to blow up the Death Star using nothing but thirty X-Wing fighters started off as an act of futility—*Star Wars.*
- Trying to throw the One Ring into the Crack of Doom using nothing but a pair of stout-hearted Hobbits started off as an act of futility—*The Lord of the Rings.*

- Doodling on the back of business cards and somehow turning it into a successful business started out as an act of
  futility—gapingvoid.com (i.e., me).

We like telling these stories because they defy the odds—and
that is what gives us hope. Hope of filling in our own "narrative
gaps." Whatever your Evil Plan might be, there has to be some
sort of sense of adventure, some sort of "triumph over adver-
sity" baked in. Otherwise, people won't want to talk about it, and
your story won't spread. People aren't merely buying your product, your Evil Plan; they are buying the story you are telling . . .
a story that's not just about you, but about them, and what they
could be.

all truly
great ideas
started life
out as an
act of
futility...

hugh

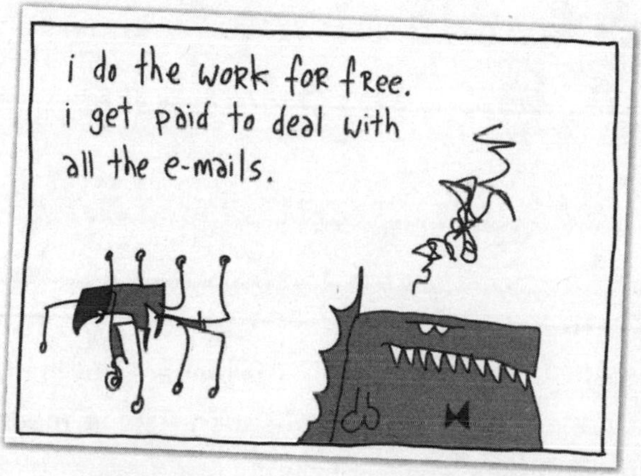
i do the work for free.
i get paid to deal with
all the e-mails.

# Success Is More Complex Than Failure

Failure's easy. Success isn't.

**RUDYARD KIPLING ONCE DESCRIBED TRIUMPH** and Disaster as "two impostors." The longer I stay in the working world, the more I start to understand what he means.

What separates success from failure (and we all experience plenty of both in our lives) is a question I've thought about a lot over the years. One day, out of nowhere, the following line hit me:

"Success is more complex than failure."

Think about it. Being a failure is a no-brainer. All you have to do is sleep till noon, get out of bed, scratch your crotch, have your morning visit to the bathroom, turn on the *Star Trek* reruns, help yourself to some breakfast (leftover pizza and a bottle of Jack Daniel's, Hurrah!), light up your first joint of the day, download some porn, and already you're well on your way.

Sure, a few inconvenient variables may enter the picture here and there to complicate an otherwise perfect day of fail—e.g., actually doing the work of figuring out who you can convince to lend you some money . . . that kind of thing. But for the most part, the day-to-day modus operandi of your average Mr. Fail is quite straightforward.

Being successful, however, is a whole different ball game. Breakfast meetings at seven a.m. Conference calls at midnight. Visiting twelve cities in five days. Fielding questions from a swarm of hostile journalists. Dealing successfully with an enraged, multimillion-dollar customer who's screaming bloody murder over something rather trivial in the grand scheme of things. Making sure there's enough money in the bank to meet the payroll of your legions of highly paid, highly effective, highly talented employees. Hundreds of unrelenting issues to deal with, all day, every day. You get the picture.

Some people can handle complexity. They're fine with that; they're fine spending their whole lives on airplanes, in meetings, and reading spreadsheets. Which is OK—different strokes for different folks and whatnot. That being said, "simple" tends to make most people more content than "complex." I think it's just the way Mother Nature made us.

had i known being
successful was
going to be this
much work, i
would've just stuck
to being a loser.

I drew this
cartoon in
Rehab....
©hugh

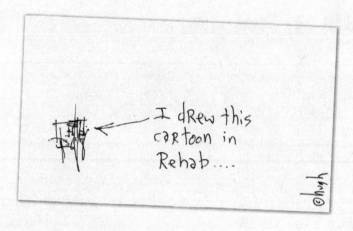

# Sleep Rough

Fortune rarely favors those with a sense of
entitlement.

**IT WAS SPRING, IN MY HOMETOWN OF ALPINE,**
Texas. I was drinking a beer at the Railroad Blues, as I often
did. Instead of the usual blues, country, and "American roots"
bands they were used to having, the group playing that evening was a young indie/power pop/alternative group from Limerick, Ireland, called "We Should Be Dead." Female lead singer
and female lead guitar, male drummer and male bass. Average
age, I'd say, was around twenty-four.

Now, Celtic indie/power pop/alternative is not exactly the
kind of music I'm into (Louis Armstrong and Beethoven are more
my cup of tea). But man, I was so impressed with these kids.
They totally played their hearts out. Not to mention, there were
a lot of cowboys and shit-kickers in the crowd that evening—not
a group you'd want to tick off. Everyone—including the cowboys

and shit-kickers—were impressed by how gutsy and fearless these kids were.

The lead singer, Tara—a tiny, skinny girl around five-two, would get off the stage in the middle of a number and walk around the crowd, singing full-blast into her mike, with these broad-shouldered cowboys wearing handlebar mustaches, ten-gallon hats, spurs, and boots, *towering* above her. Like I said, fearless. So even if the music was a bit alien compared with what people were normally used to, they still got a lot of people whoopin' and a'hollerin' that night. It was a great show. Months later, people were still talking about it.

I got talking to their manager—a stocky, Irish dude in his forties. It turns out, though they were now on tour, they hadn't planned it that way. They had originally only come over for the big music festival in Austin, Texas—South by Southwest—and were planning to return to Ireland right afterward.

Then somehow while at SXSW the manager made some new connections, and the next thing you know, the band was headed west to California, ready and willing to play in every dive bar and dance hall en route that would let them—sometimes only for tips. Buying an old van; throwing their instruments, amplifiers, and sleeping bags in the back; living on a few bucks a day plus gas money; sleeping rough if they had to.

And they were going to keep on doing it till they had spent their last nickel, till they had burned their last drop of gas. Only then, and not before, would they fly back home.

Sure, they could have gone back to Ireland after SXSW

instead and continued being a regular fixture around the local pub 'n' club circuit. But they wanted to bust out of that routine—and here was their chance. Not a huge chance, but a chance nonetheless. And they were going for it, no questions asked. Like Anna, the equally tiny-skinny lead guitarist told me in her cute little Limerick accent, "We don't want to go home. We want to keep doing this forever."

Would you be willing to put in that kind of effort and commitment to make your Evil Plan a success? How willing to "sleep rough" are you? Are you that brave? Am I?

FOLLOW-UP: A couple of years later, at the time of this book going to print, I am happy to report that We Should Be Dead is still in America, playing mostly around Los Angeles and keeping really busy. God bless 'em! . . .

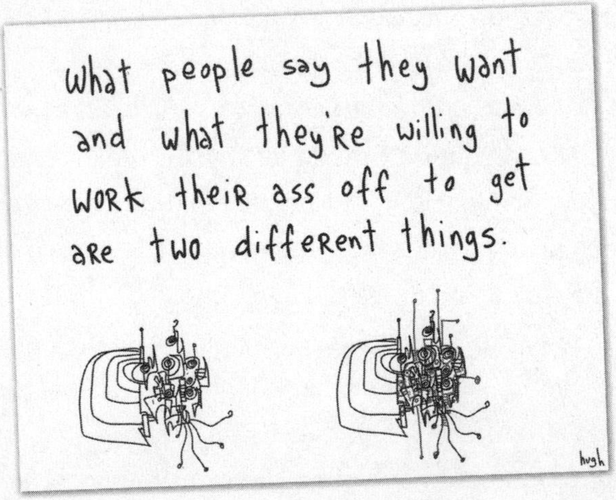
what people say they want and what they're willing to work their ass off to get are two different things.
hugh

george is
changing the
system from
the inside!!

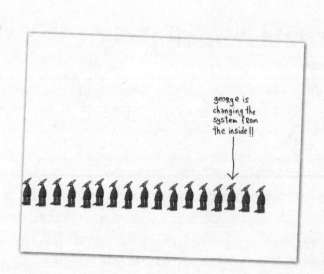

# Create "Social"

Your Evil Plan has to have some sort of "sociality" baked in, or else it will fail.

**BOINGBOING.NET IS ONE OF MY FAVORITE** blogs. All that neato, geeked-out techie stuff has also made it one of the most widely read blogs in the world, and deservedly so.

So why is it so popular? The most obvious answer, "great content," is a no-brainer. Of course it has great content. People wouldn't read it if it didn't.

But "great content" is only half the story. The other half is just as important, though a little more subtle. And what is that?

Short answer: "sociality."

It's not just that BoingBoing's content is fun to *read*. It is. It's also that BoingBoing's content is fun to *share*.

"Wow. What a cool article about Japanese nanorobots. I

think I'll e-mail it along to my friends at work. Better yet, I think I'll mention it to my hundreds of Twitter followers. Hell, I'll even blog about it. . . ."

BoingBoing has a lot of "sociality" baked in—that is, its content makes for great "social objects." And their blog posts are great "sharing devices."

We are primates. We are social creatures. We like to socialize. And we socialize around objects. BoingBoing cranks out "social objects" by the ton, in the form of cool blog posts that we can effortlessly pass along to our friends.

And that's where the true value of BoingBoing lies. It acts as a "sharing device," allowing you to connect with others. Will sending your old college buddy Bob a link to a cool BoingBoing post about culturally subversive Detroit photographers permanently change his life for the better? Probably not.

But giving you something that allows you and Bob to socialize with each other ("Cool post, dude!") digs deep into what really matters to us primates: socializing. Sharing ourselves with fellow members of our species.

And what's true for blogs like BoingBoing is true for any other product. Again, it's not what the product *does* that matters to us so much, it's how we socialize around it that matters. This is why the iPhone has been so successful. Sure, we like having all those cool apps, but being able to talk about and recommend cool apps to our friends, that's what we are genetically hardwired to like even more.

So ask yourself, how are people going to "socialize" around your Evil Plan? How is "sociality" baked in? How is your Evil Plan a "social object"? These are questions you should take seriously.

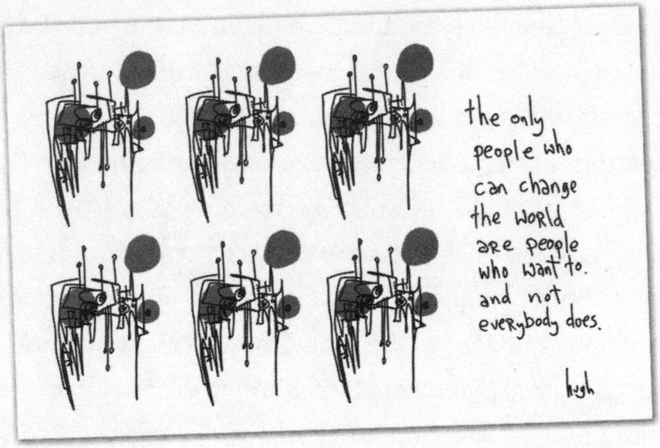
the only
people who
can change
the WORLD
are people
who want to.
and not
everybody does.
hugh

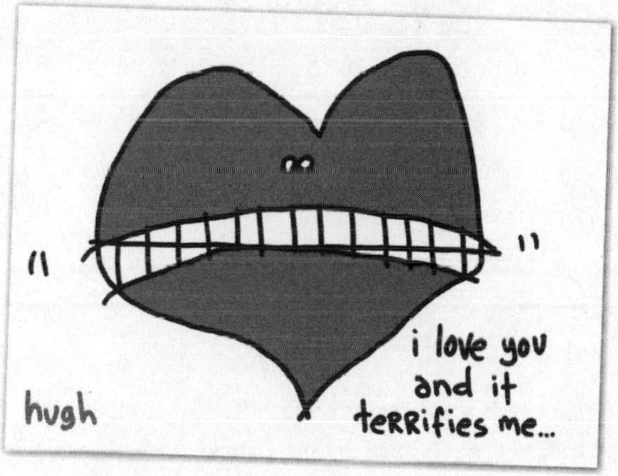
" "
i love you
and it
terrifies me...
hugh

# Create Snowballs

Evil Plans are like snowballs, they require
"Random Acts of Traction."

**"RANDOM ACTS OF TRACTION" IS A PHRASE I**
use a lot these days.

It seems to be the story of my life.

I put stuff out there—cartoons, prints, a book, a blog post . . .
whatever. Some of it works, some of it goes nowhere.

A decade of pretty successful writing and cartooning later,
and I *still* have no way of predicting what will work and what
will fail.

Who knew my first book, *Ignore Everybody*, would be a
bestseller? Who knew the phrase "social object" would enter
the lexicon of mainstream marketing simply by me rabbiting
on about it on my blog ad nauseam? Who knew *"Wolf vs.
Sheep"* would be my most popular-selling fine-art print? Who
knew all these things would gain "Random Acts of Traction"?

Certainly not me.

The great Doc Searls, coauthor of *The Cluetrain Manifesto,* one of my all-time favorite business books, said it on his blog a few years ago much better than I ever could:

> Tell ya what. I'm fifty-seven years old, and I've been pushing large rocks for short distances up a lot of hills, for a long time. Now, with blogging, I get to roll snowballs down hills. Some don't go very far. But some get pretty big once they start rolling.
>
> See, each snowball grows as others link to the original idea, and add their own thoughts and ideas. By the time the snowball gets big enough to have some impact, it really isn't my idea any more.
>
> Anyway, at this point in my life I'd rather roll snowballs than push rocks.

I think anyone who, like me, makes a living even partly via blogs and social media inherently understands the snowball metaphor and will therefore understand "Random Acts of Traction."

My friend James Governor, a technology analyst (twitter .com/monkchips), certainly understands this. Since he and his business partners can only realistically execute 10 percent of their ideas, they don't seem to mind giving away the remaining 90 percent for free, via their blogs. If one of their free ideas gets "Random Acts of Traction" and ends up spreading around the Internet, it's great PR for their businesses. It eventually leads to conversations. Conversations that eventually lead to paid gigs.

Evil Plans like James's, of course, only work if you can make your "snowballs" quickly and inexpensively enough. If you spend too much time worrying about it, you lose. If you try to control where the snowballs go after you've released them down the hill, you lose.

Without understanding that a lot of random traction is baked in to the equation, Evil Plans wouldn't be allowed to happen.

at least
i tried.
you?
hugh

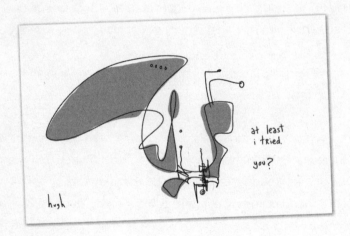

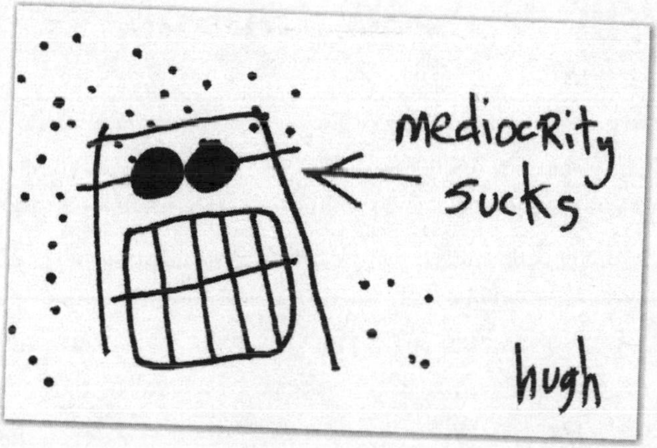
mediocrity
sucks
hugh

# Avoid Dinosaurspeak

Hugh MacLeod's gapingvoid.com is the perfect website to get your daily blogging fix. Filled to the brim with hilarious cartoons, it also offers timely and insightful commentary on the new realities of adverting and marketing. Indeed, some people would say it's just not the blogosphere without gapingvoid.com to enhance their quality blogging experience. Start your day the switched-on way: Subscribe to get gapingvoid.com on your RSS feeder today!

**I WROTE THE PRECEDING PARAGRAPH TO** illustrate the intellectual bankruptcy of what I call "Dinosaurspeak." Ninety-five percent of marketing talks to us that way. That rather sociopathic combination of being completely focused on customer benefit and yet completely selfish at the same time.

And yeah, if it doesn't work for my shtick, it ain't going to work with your Evil Plan either.

What is interesting to me is that this style of "marketing-speak" was pretty universal only a few years ago, which in Internet time was like the Mesozoic era. Sure, you had a few mavericks out there stirring things up, but most external business communication was pretty much stuck in fire-hose mode.

But when, thanks to the Internet, markets become smarter and faster than the companies servicing said markets, language changes and Dinosaurspeak must face extinction. Of course it does. Talk like a human being, not like one of Stalin's apparatchiks. People are hardwired to respond favorably to that.

have you hugged your client today?

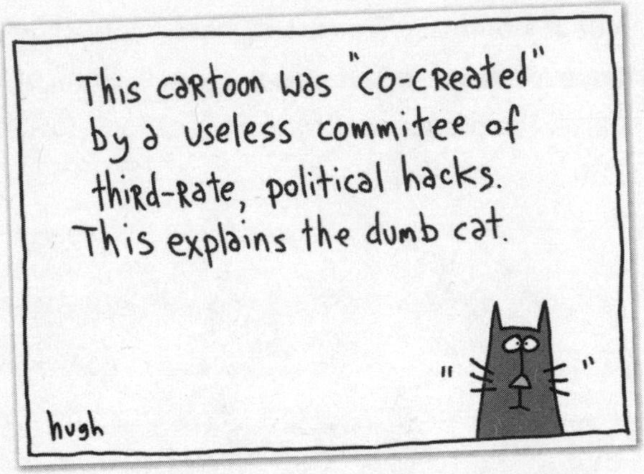
This cartoon was "co-created" by a useless commitee of third-rate, political hacks. This explains the dumb cat.
" "
hugh

# Find Your "Moment"

The things that define us and our business can be surprisingly instantaneous.

**SIMON THORNHILL IS A GOOD FRIEND OF MINE.** He and his lovely wife own the Troubadour in London, the legendary restaurant and nightclub. Jimi Hendrix and Bob Dylan played there, back when they were still unknown musicians. The Thornhills bought the place from the previous owners a few years ago.

Before that, Simon was an officer in the Scots Guards—a highly respected Scottish regiment in the British Army. He's tough as nails, but a bit of a hippie, too. If you ever visit Earl's Court, look him up. He's terrific company.

I don't know what we were talking about that night at the bar, but somehow the conversation got on to the subject of young Army officers. Some of the kids I went to high school with in Edinburgh ended up joining regiments right after finishing their exams, so Simon's previous life wasn't a world completely unknown to me. These kids sign up at age seventeen or eighteen, take their two-year training at Sandhurst (the UK equivalent to West Point), maybe do a stint at university, and the next thing you know, they're in the field, armed to the teeth and giving orders to experienced, tough-as-nails sergeants and corporals twice their age.

I don't know about you, but I would find that *really* intimidating. Those young kids must have *cojones,* I'll tell you that. I was telling Simon how terrifying I thought it must be, to be a kid barely out of school, with all the men *far* more experienced than you under your command, holding you in the traditional squaddies' contempt reserved for all new, young officers.

"Yes, that certainly happens," said Simon. "But then you finally have what they call in the British Army 'The Moment.' The moment when you stop trying to be your men's new best friend and actually start to lead them. That's when you *really* become an officer—and not when you first receive your commission.

"That happened to me when we were on a night exercise. I had only left Sandhurst a few months previously. Things were going terribly wrong, nobody was doing their jobs. Everything was in shambles. Finally I had my 'Moment.' I just pulled my finger out and firmly said to the men, 'I'm in command, you're not; you will do as I say or I will have you all up on charges, boys. Now fucking go do your jobs.' Somehow they knew I wasn't joking.

"And so they went off and obeyed their orders, without any fuss. A few of them were easily ten or fifteen years older than me. . . . The thing is, they might not think much of the young kid giving them orders at first, but at the same time, soldiers do want to be led."

As with Simon, I think we all need to have that "Moment" eventually. That moment when we stop futzing around and actually start behaving like proper adults. That moment when we actually start acting like officers in command of our own lives.

I remember mine. I didn't think too much about it at the time, but over the years I realized just how important it ended up being.

I was a young freelance advertising creative, living in London, meeting a girlfriend for a drink at my regular Soho watering hole, the Coach and Horses.

The bar was crowded and noisy that evening. The barmaid was a young, pretty Chinese gal who'd only been in the country a short while. She spoke pretty good English, but not great.

I asked the barmaid for a glass of wine for my friend; and for me, a gin and tonic with *four* slices of lime. I even held up four fingers to help make it clear to her.

So the poor barmaid ended up bringing me back five drinks—my friend's glass of wine, with four *gin and tonics,* each with a *single* slice of lime. Oops. We're talking about a round that I suppose easily exceeded the U.S. equivalent of thirty or forty dollars. The poor girl got the order bassackwards.

A simple misunderstanding, I guess. Plus, like I said, her English wasn't very good. I told the barmaid about the mix-up. "No, I asked for a *single* gin and tonic with *four* slices of lime."

Up until that moment, like any young pub drinker, I probably would then have just asked the barmaid to take the surplus three drinks away and add more lime slices to the remaining drink. Easy. But I didn't.

Instead, I asked her, "Will this mistake be coming out of your wages?"

"Yes," she replied.

I already knew enough about the bar's owner to know that she wasn't lying.

The thing is, unlike here in the United States, the people working in London pubs don't work for tips—mainly because nobody really tips there. You might get two or three pounds a night if you're lucky. They get paid by the hour, usually minimum wage, in one of the most expensive cities in the world. Hence London bartenders tend to be really, really poor. The mistake the barmaid made would be, for her, extremely expensive. Two or three hours' wages or so, maybe even more.

"Never mind," I said. "Just put three more limes in one of the glasses, and I'll pay for the other three gins as well." Which I did.

Then it was just a matter of keeping one of the drinks for myself and finding three other random people in the bar who were not above accepting free gin and tonics from a total stranger with an American accent. This being the Coach and Horses, that took all of twenty seconds. "Cheers, Mate!"

A year or two before that, I probably would've just allowed the young barmaid to take the hit. "You made the mistake, not me, not my problem" is the reasoning.

But London was being kind to me at the time; life was good. Meanwhile this young Chinese girl was living thousands of miles away from her family, and probably doing so very close to the poverty line. So I chose to take the hit instead of her. I know I didn't have to, I was perfectly within my rights not to, but . . .

I didn't want to be that kind of person anymore. I really didn't.

So that was my "Moment."

And every successful enterprise I've ever started or been involved with, had its "Moment" at some point as well. That moment where you finally decide to not cut corners, to not make excuses, even if you can get away with it. Even if 99 percent of other businesses wouldn't have bothered.

These moments are gold dust, they really are.

Has your Evil Plan had its "Moment" yet? If not, what can you do to make it happen sooner? Serious question.

*(Hint: You can't force the "Moment" to arrive. All you can do is "Decide." Think about it.)*

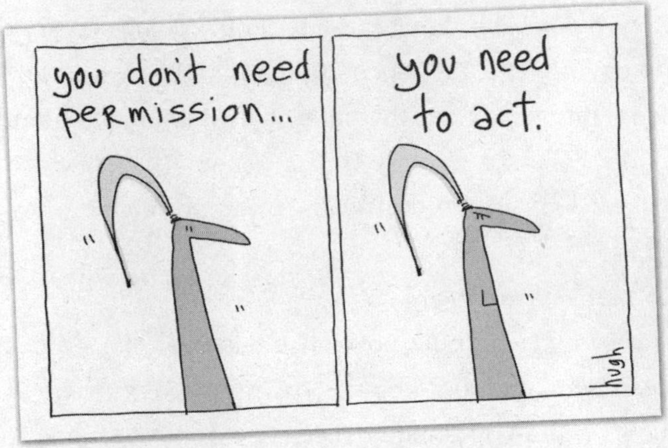
you don't need permission...
you need to act.
hugh

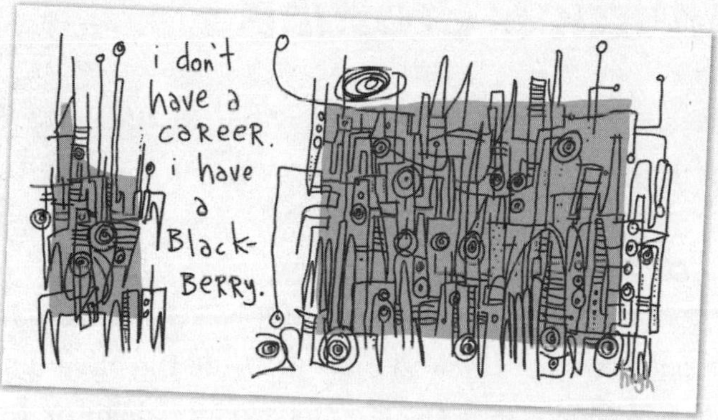
i don't have a career. i have a Black-Berry.

# Embrace Crofting

"Crofting" is a great metaphor for the new world of work we now see emerging.

**MY PATERNAL GRANDFATHER WAS A SCOTTISH** Highland "crofter." He lived on a croft—that is, a very small holding of land with a small cottage on it—where he raised sheep and cows, cut his own hay, and grew oats, turnips, and potatoes. I used to spend my summers there as a boy. We were very close.

Probably the most famous crofters are the ones from the Isle of Harris, who spend their winters indoors, hand-weaving Harris Tweed so they can sell it to all the top fashion houses in the world like Burberry and Ralph Lauren. A revered little traditional cottage industry, indeed.

Crofting is a good life, but not a very financially rewarding one. It's very self-sufficient, though. The interesting thing for me, looking back, is that crofters never did "just one thing."

Every day they had something else going on. One day it might be looking after their sheep. The next it might be a job working on the roads for the local council. I knew one crofter who drove the mail van. Another who ran the local post office. They would do their jobs, but after work they'd still have their sheep, cows, and potatoes to tend to. It's the same with the Harris Tweed weavers, too. They keep busy.

The other advantage of crofting is, when the outside world is not hiring at the moment, you can always live on lamb, oats, turnips, and potatoes indefinitely if you have to. Not fun, maybe, but at least you can survive till times get better, which they always do. . . .

As my dad is fond of reminding me, I seem to have inherited the crofting mentality. I *don't* like waking up in the morning and doing the same thing every day. I *do* like having all these different balls in the air—cartooning, painting, consulting, writing, marketing, blogging, etc. Sure, part of me would like nothing better than to just "retire to the desert and make paintings," but another part of me likes all of the running around in different directions. Even if all of this running around *does* get tiring, an endless torrent of stuff needing to get done.

The traditional Highland crofter is pretty much a thing of the past. As my uncle, a crofter like his father before him, recently quipped, "We just farm manila envelopes now" (farm subsidies from the European bureaucrats tend to arrive in manila envelopes). But since the BigCorp job-for-life is becoming a thing of the past, expect to see more "crofters" out there, even though it's no longer sheep and potatoes we're selling. I think it's a sweet little term that conveys a lot, especially to those of us who seem to have a built-in aversion to salaried positions in other people's companies. Don't you?

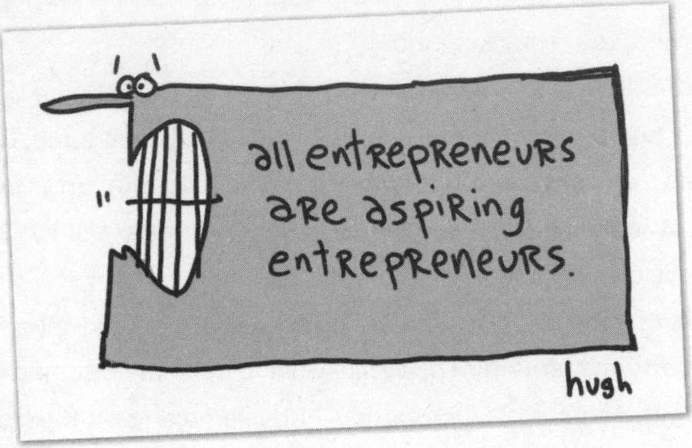
all entrepreneurs
are aspiring
entrepreneurs.
hugh

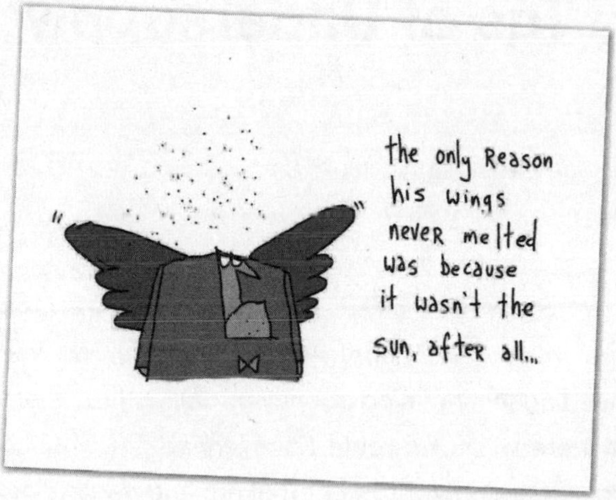
the only Reason
his wings
never melted
was because
it wasn't the
sun, after all...

# The Tao of Undersupply

The biggest problem in the Western world is oversupply. Don't let it be yours.

**FOR EVERY MID-LEVEL MANAGING JOB OPENING** up, there are scores of people willing and able. For every company needing to hire an ad agency or design firm, there's dozens out there, willing and able. For every person wanting to buy a new car, there are tons of car makers and dealers out there. I could go on and on.

I could also go on about how many good people I know who are caught in oversupplied markets, and how every day they wake up feeling chilled to the bone with dread and unease. Advertising and media folk are classic examples.

So maybe the thing is to get into "The Tao of Undersupply."

If only 100 people want to buy your widgets, then just make 90 widgets. If only 1,000, make 900. If only 10 million, make 9 million. It isn't rocket science, but it takes discipline.

It also requires you to stop making the same stuff as other people. This requires originality and invention. Harder than it looks.

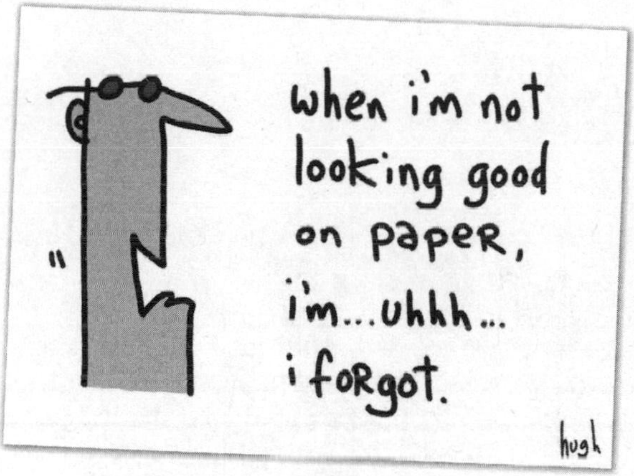
"
when i'm not
looking good
on paper,
i'm...uhhh...
i forgot.
hugh

90% of
corporate
life is
feigning
interest.

hugh

# Don't Be "Middle-Seat Guy"

Too many people are in the business of trying to sell what people don't actually want. Don't be one of them.

**ONE OF MY PET PEEVES WHEN TRAVELING (AND** I travel quite a bit these days) is when I get assigned to the middle seat on an airplane.

We all know why; we all know middle seats are uncomfortable and nasty. We all know that they basically suck.

The good airline folk will tell me they've already booked all the window and aisle seats. They've only got middle seats left. Sorry, they say.

Which always makes me say to myself, "Those middle seats shouldn't be on the airplane in the first place."

Middle seats are, to me, a product of a different era. They were invented when the first long-distance jet airliners came around, the Boeing 707, the VC10, and so on. Before that they just had aisle and window seats.

A lot of airplanes we use today—the Boeing 747, the Boeing 737, for example—were designed before the airline industry was deregulated, when air travel was still *really* expensive. When people had far fewer choices. When people flew a lot less often.

But the world is changing. JetBlue currently buys long, skinny airplanes to make getting rid of the middle seat economically viable. But they're a new airline. Older, larger, more established airlines are still beholden to their old, fat airplanes, stuffed to the brim with middle seats.

It won't happen overnight, but there will come a time when offering your airline customers a middle seat will be tantamount to economic suicide, at least on U.S. domestic flights.

Because people simply don't want middle seats. They never did. And they'll gladly take their business over to someone who doesn't have them on offer.

This middle-seat-free day will be great news for us customers when it arrives, of course. But not if you're "Middle-Seat Guy."

Middle-Seat Guy is the guy at the airline whose job it is to figure out the middle seats—how many of them they can cram onto a plane, how to sell middle seats as efficiently as possible to people who never wanted them to begin with, and so on.

So imagine some day not too far in the future, he's suddenly out of a job. People aren't buying middle seats anymore and suddenly the world has no more use for his services. He's at home, he's bitter, he feels personally betrayed by the airline that employed him for twenty years. His life sucks and he's hitting the bottle before noon.

Whether we're talking about airlines or any other kind of business, the fact is, the Internet has made it *much* harder to sell your customers metaphorical "middle seats." And the punishment for trying to get away with it is getting more and more swift and severe. Because the consumer will answer back, equally swiftly and severely:

No, we don't want to give your law practice $7,500 to create a living will in order to help you pay off your six-figure student loans from law school. We'd much rather download something off the Internet that does the same job for $99.99.

No, we don't want you interrupting our favorite reality TV show and making us watch your commercials so you can show us your well-crafted, multimillion-dollar marketing message about how wonderful your client's automobiles are. We'd much rather get the skinny from an online forum.

No, we don't want to buy your generic, cardboard-tasting, mass-produced cookies from the local convenience store; we'd rather order some online from this Buddhist monk weirdo lumberjack in Montana who makes—by hand and in tiny batches—*the most amazing* cookies ever.

No, we don't want to buy your $25 bottle of nasty, overpriced sulfur-saturated Californian vinegar. We'd rather buy this great little $10 Australian red Shiraz that this cool wine blogger turned us on to.

I don't know what's going to happen to this economy in the long run. I do know, however, that a lot of Middle-Seat Guys are going to be suddenly out of work, with *zero* idea about what to do next. I hope that doesn't include you.

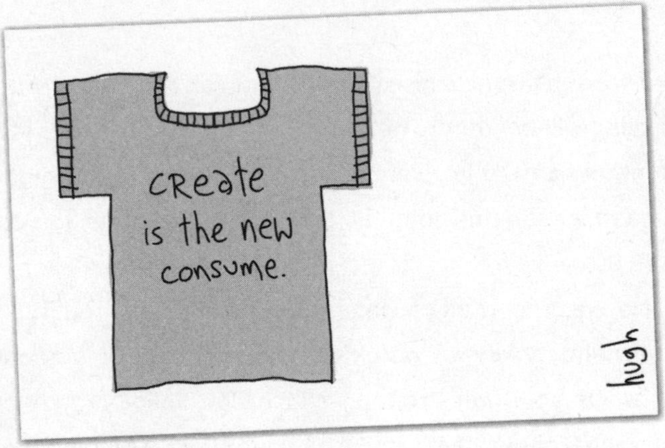
create
is the new
consume.
hugh

china
japan
korea
india
TAIWAN
hawaii
Australia
seattle
canada
wasteland
new york
hipsters
wasteland
mexico
brazil
L.A.
nice vacation spot
london
EUROPE
iRAQ
afghanistan
dubai
africa
silicon valley map
hugh

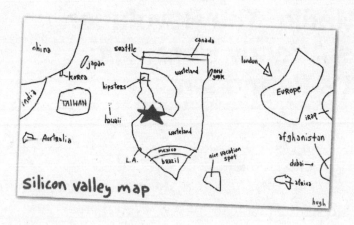

# Cheap, Easy, Global Media: The Revolution Is Already Here, and It's Permanent

"So forget about blogs and bloggers and blogging and focus on this—the cost and difficulty of publishing absolutely anything, by anyone, into a global medium, just got a whole lot lower. And the effects of that increased pool of potential producers is going to be vast."

—CLAY SHIRKY, 2004

**FOR A CARTOONIST, I GOT INTO BLOGGING** relatively early, in May 2001.

It was a format I understood right away, for no other reason than when compared to the price of building a regular website back then, it was cheap and easy. And since I was *really* broke at the time, for someone wanting to get their work online and seen by people, it was a godsend.

Then around 2005, back when blogs became the hot news story for journalists everywhere, Clay Shirky's words above came in handy. It kept things in perspective during blogging's short-lived media frenzy.

But things changed soon enough, of course. The blogger's reign at the top of the new media food chain soon came to an end. At the time of writing this, Twitter is the hot new website that everyone's talking about incessantly, with Foursquare quickly coming up from behind. A year or two ago it was Facebook. The year before that It was MySpace. And hey, remember Friendster? Doubtless something else will come along next year—it always does.

But what blogging represented back in 2004 is never going away, save for the total extinction of the human race. I'm not just talking about blogs, I'm talking about something much bigger. It's here forever. It's not a fad. This is what Shirky was talking about: cheap, easy, global media.

Get used to living with it. Get used to working with it. Avoid it at your peril.

give me
hot
hot
internet
all day
long!
hugh

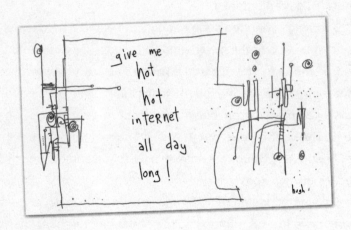

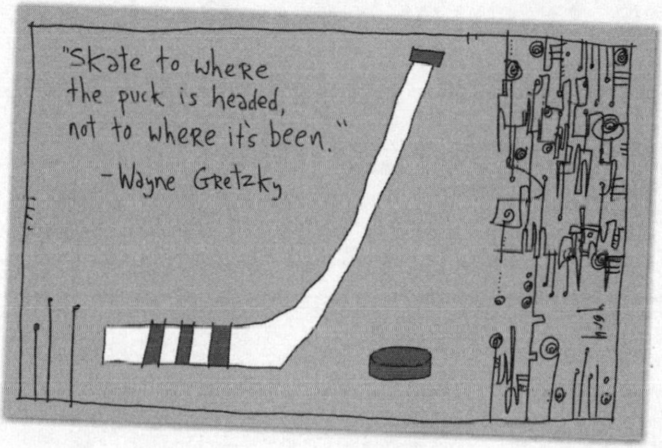
"Skate to where the puck is headed, not to where it's been."
-Wayne Gretzky

# "The Twenty": Control the Conversation by Improving the Conversation

Doc Searls, when trying to articulate how marketing works on the Internet (or not), famously quipped, "All markets are conversations." From your standpoint, that means you have to start "owning the conversation" of whatever space your business occupies.

**"CONVERSATION OWNERSHIP" ISN'T ROCKET** science. Owning a conversation simply means that regardless of what enterprise you're in, the higher up the food chain/ social hierarchy you go, the more likely they're talking about you and not about somebody else.

I would suggest that, right this minute, you make a list of the twenty or so people in your space who matter *the most*. Then ask yourself, who on this list is actually reading your stuff, actually follows what you're up to, actually knows that you exist?

If most of the people on the list are checking you out, everyone else will follow eventually. If they're not, then you've got a wee bit of a marketing problem.

How do you get your stuff on the radar screen of "The Twenty"? By creating brilliant stuff. By creating brilliant stuff that "speaks" to the market in a way it has never been spoken to before. If your stuff is different enough that it changes "the conversation" of your market for the better, other folk will notice, even the Big Boys. "Improve the conversation by improving the language." All great marketing breakthroughs are evolutions of language.

The Web has made kicking ass easier to achieve, and Mediocrity harder to sustain. Mediocrity now howls in protest.

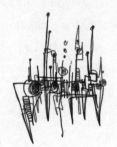

choosing an easy life
RaRely ends up with
much of either.

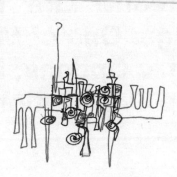

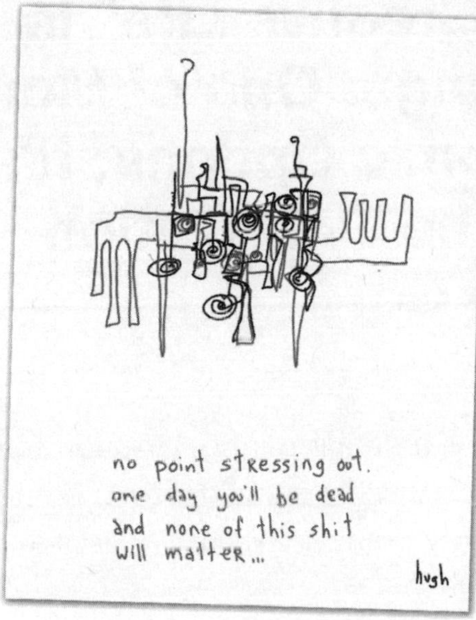

no point stressing out.
one day you'll be dead
and none of this shit
will matter...

hugh

# The "Creative Life" Is No Longer One of Many Economic Options; It's Now the Only Option We've Got

If you were expecting a long, thousand-word explanation to follow this chapter's title, you'd be mistaken. The point is so glaringly obvious, it doesn't need it.

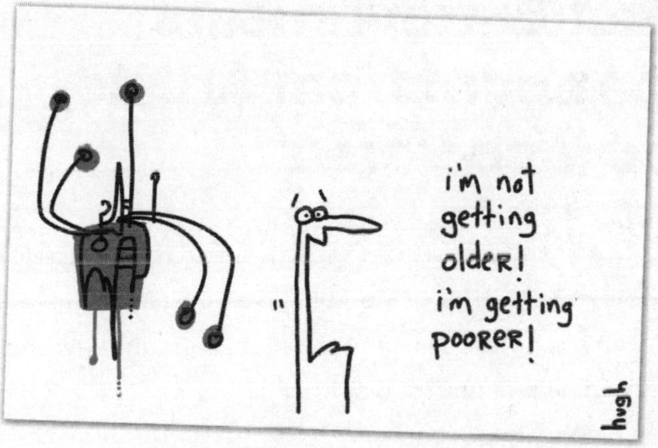
i'm not getting older! i'm getting poorer!
hugh

# What Entrepreneurs Can Learn from Artists, and Vice Versa

**I REALLY LIKED THE TITLE OF THIS CHAPTER** when I first wrote it. I even had plans to turn it into a major blog post with a long list of useful, lucid pointers that my readers would find helpful and/or inspiring.

But nothing happened.

The line just floated there in limbo for weeks, almost mockingly. . . .

Every time I tried to write this "useful, lucid" blog post, I ended up hating what I had written.

Of course I did.

Why?

Because the thought is redundant.

In their own way, all artists are entrepreneurs, and all entrepreneurs are artists.

Though their tools and products may differ, both entrepreneurs and artists are in the same game—the making and selling of work that is personally and emotionally important to them.

"Artist." "Entrepreneur." They're just words. What's far more interesting is not what we create, but how we create it, *why* we create it.

Life is short.

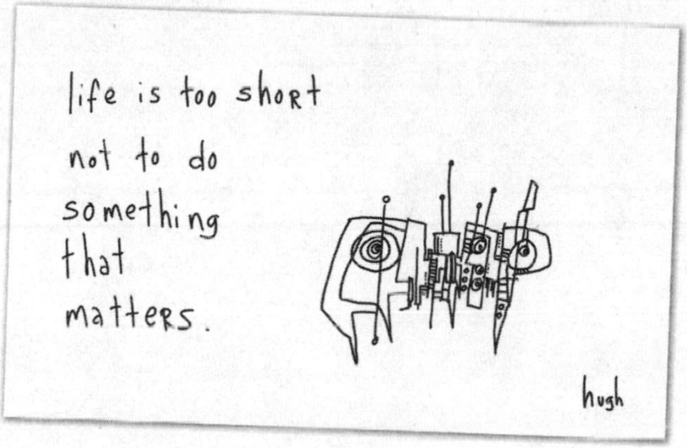
life is too short
not to do
something
that
matters.
hugh

the trouble with
New York
is
everyone
is using
the same
source code.

hugh

# No, You Can't Have It All

Especially if you want to do something that matters.

**ONE THING THAT CAUSES FAR TOO MUCH OF** the proverbial "quiet desperation" in modern society is the relentless pursuit of "having it all."

*"Who says you can't have it all?"* were the lyrics of annoyingly upbeat TV jingle from the 1980s.

This campaign for Michelob Lite beer tritely asked the question "Who says you can't love your work and leave it too?" as a sly substitute for the question "Who says you can't get great, satisfying taste in a beer that also happens to be kinda light and watery?"

I remember seeing the ad as a kid. Some yuppie who looked good in a suit, looked good in a corporate office, but also looked pretty good on the basketball court with his buddies, and who also looked good wielding an electric guitar surrounded by an admiring group of ladies. Loving his work and leaving it too, as the jingle reaches its triumphant climax: *"Oh yes you caaaaan . . . have it all!"* How soul stirring. Tolstoy or Beethoven would be proud etc., etc.

If you search around for it on the Internet, you'll find that the campaign wasn't that successful, ultimately.

Of course it wasn't. Why? Because as we all know, Life isn't like that.

How many PhD's have quit their stellar careers in academia to go play for the NFL? How many NBA stars, after they retired from basketball, go off to run a division of IBM?

The sacrifices are utterly, utterly enormous to be the best in the world at something—or even *really* good at it. "Have it all?" Are you insane?

Everyone knows this.

Everyone except Michelob Lite back in 1987, it seems. Which is why, twenty-plus years after declaring their ability to be all things to all people, that brand is still struggling, trying hard to be something—*anything*—other than unexceptional. Luckily for the Michelob Brewing Company, some of their other brands have been doing quite well lately—Michelob Ultra, for example. So at least they learned a few lessons along the way. I wish them well.

Of course, this "have it all," sacrifice-free attitude isn't just the domain of ho-hum beer brands. It's the domain of ho-hum individual careers, as well. You can only hope that yours is not one of them.

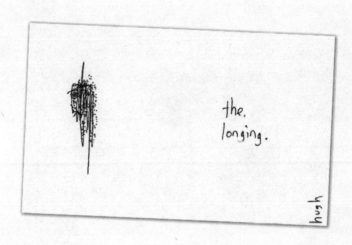

the.
longing.

hugh

MEDIOCRITY
LOVES
SLAVERY.

# If Your Boss Won't Let You Articulate Your Evil Plan During Company Hours, Quit

"My boss won't let me" is a terrible excuse for not getting on with building your own Evil Plan, within reasonable confines of your job. A good boss wants her employees to have their own sense of sovereignty and destiny. Why on earth would you tolerate a boss who didn't?

I ONCE HAD A BOSS WHO DIDN'T LIKE THE fact that I had a blog. Especially when I blogged about stuff that was relative to our industry. "The company brand must speak with one voice," he endlessly kept insisting. Yes, I know.

Actually, the reality was that *he* wanted to be the "one voice." He wanted all the credit and all the rewards. He didn't mind me putting words into his mouth—stuff I had written—just as long as the outside world gave him all the credit. But he didn't want me in any other role besides subservient, nowheres-ville wage slave. He fought tooth and nail to keep me from ever becoming a rainmaker for the company, something he wanted all for himself.

I left the job a few months later. I was glad to leave, frankly.

The story actually has a happy ending. Though I had no intention of quitting blogging, to deflect the heat the boss was giving me, I decided to stop writing about our industry for a while. I decided instead to write about a different subject altogether.

Not quite sure what to write about, I just started digging into my past experiences and started writing a series of blog posts on the subject of creativity, using what I had learned from all those years of cartooning. This series ended up being read online by a lot of people and then went on to become my first book, *Ignore Everybody,* which went on to become a *Wall Street Journal* bestseller and a 2009 Top Ten Editor's Pick at Amazon.

Last time I heard, my former boss's situation hasn't changed much. He's still hacking away in buzzword-infested mediocrity, his "Speak with One Voice" shtick still being completely dis-regarded by anyone who matters in the industry.

Schadenfreude.

IF YOU CAN
EXPRESS YOUR
SOUL, THE REST
CEASES TO
MATTER.

the optimist!

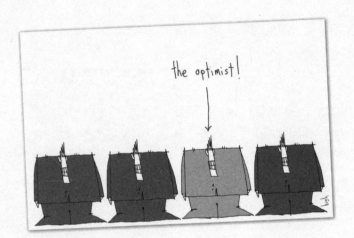

# Get Other People to Hate You

The bad news is, the better your Evil Plan, the more people are going to hate it.

**THE GOOD NEWS IS, THE BETTER YOUR EVIL** Plan, the more people are going to love it.

In Gustave Flaubert's great literary masterpiece, *Madame Bovary,* the narrator describes Monsieur Bovary (the husband that our heroine eventually cuckolds) with the most damning description I've ever read of a fictional character: "He offended no more than he pleased."

In getting us to identify with Madame Bovary and dislike Monsieur Bovary, Flaubert was very clever. He made sure that Monsieur Bovary wasn't evil or a sociopath; he just made him a conventional, boring, inoffensive, *completely uninspiring* member of the middle classes—completely aligned with and beholden to nineteenth-century, respectable French society.

And we couldn't help but despise him for it. Because he wasn't interestingly evil, nor was he fabulously fantastic and sensational. He was just as human as the rest of us, he had just made a conscious decision to emasculate his own humanity for the sake of social standing—something we're all very capable of doing ourselves.

Walk into any supermarket and you'll see again a similar phenomenon. Aisle after aisle full of products that most people, frankly, don't really give two hoots about. Sure, there might be a perfectly good brand of paper towel or breakfast cereal, but at the end of the day, like Monsieur Bovary, they offend no more than they please. And so how much do people care? Answer: diddly-squat.

And go visit these products' corporate headquarters and you'll meet their human equivalent. Aisle after aisle of people in cubes. Sure, they'll be perfectly nice, educated, polite and all; they'll be efficient and good at their jobs and all; but how many people would care if one of them lost his job tomorrow? Answer: no one.

But once your Evil Plan starts getting traction, you'll start noticing a much more polarized world begin to emerge. People who *love* what you do, and people who *utterly despise* it.

Why such strong feelings? Why the emotions? You're just doing your thing, they're just doing their thing, so what's the big deal?

Answer: Because a lot of people aren't actually doing *their* own thing. They're just trying to pay their bills, living paycheck to paycheck, payroll to payroll, promotion to promotion.

To some of these people your example will give them hope: "I may just be schlepping now, but *one day* I'll leave this cubicle farm and *then* go do something amazing!" Those people will love you and buy into your Evil Plan. Hell, some of them will even give you money.

But some people will hate your Evil Plan too, for no real reason. Envy? Jealousy? Of course. Your example is not giving them hope, your example is just making them more aware of their own issues and inadequacies. And maybe it's easier for them to attack you than attack their own demons.

In Internet circles, we call these people "trolls" or "haters." They're easy to spot, mainly because they're everywhere.

Sure, the haters are a pain, especially at first, when you're not used to this kind of treatment.

But they do serve a purpose. If you were just schleppping along like they were, they wouldn't bother going after you, their sights would be turned elsewhere.

Ergo, the haters are a sign that you're doing something right. So you probably want to get other people to hate you eventually—that is, the right kind of people. In some ways, they might actually end up helping you define your mission to others, more than the people who actually love you.

Yes, it's so worth it. . . .

getting a lot of people to hate you is easy—
all you have to do is become really successful at doing
something you love.

high

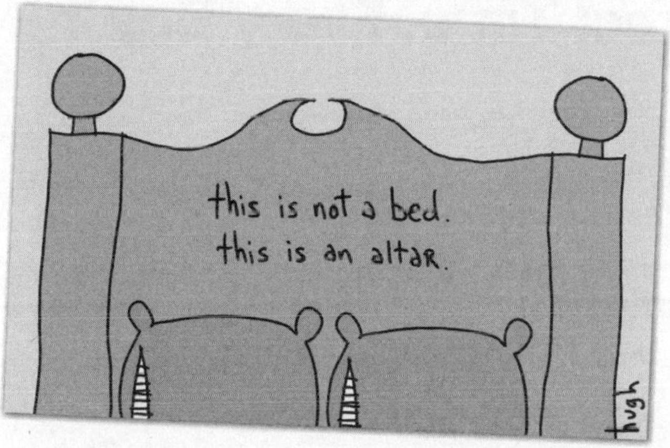
this is not a bed.
this is an altar.
hugh

# Steal Time, Every Day

Napoleon once said, "I can always regain lost territory. A single second, never."

**TRUER WORDS WERE NEVER SPOKEN.**

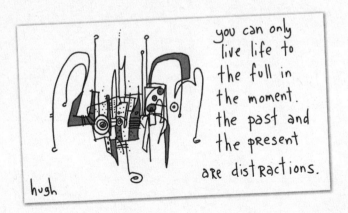

you can only live life to the full in the moment. the past and the present are distractions.

hugh

I AWOKE FROM
THE NIGHTMARE
ALL COMPLACENCY
DEAD.

hugh

# The Pressure to "Not Be Shit"

Stop whining and get used to it. It's never going away.

**MY OLD CHILDHOOD FRIEND, DAVID MACKENZIE,** is a critically acclaimed film director. He has made award-winning features and worked with famous actors like Ewan McGregor, Tilda Swinton, Ashton Kutcher, and Sir Ian McKellen. His first big feature, *Young Adam*, was produced by the same guy who produced *The Last Emperor*. He's respected in the business, let's just say that.

He's made about nine or ten films in the last decade. He's been busy. He's been in demand.

The last time he was out here visiting me in West Texas, we were drinking a beer at Harry's Tinaja, my local watering hole. Just enjoying the evening light and the pleasant company around us.

"It doesn't get any easier," he says. "No matter how much money the last film made, how many awards the last film won . . . *everything* about this business is hard."

He takes a sip of beer.

"The pressure 'to not be shit,'" he continues, "is here forever. The only thing you can do is decide how you want to deal with it."

Your Evil Plan won't make your life any easier. In fact, it'll probably make it harder. But knowing that beforehand will make the experience of being alive, here and now, far richer and more enjoyable. I happen to think it's worth it.

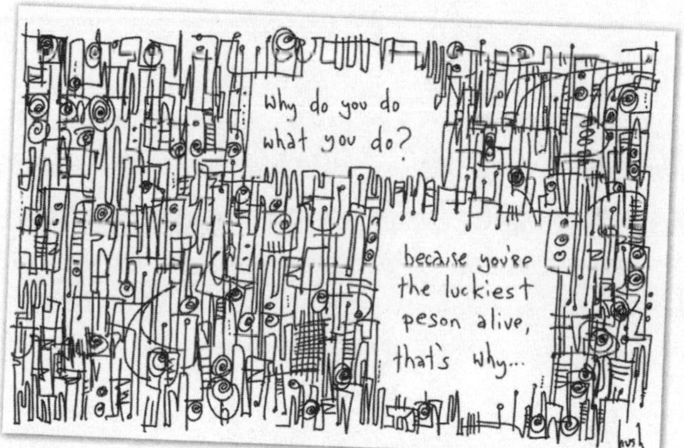
why do you do
what you do?
because you're
the luckiest
peson alive,
that's why...
hugh

i wish my
heart was
bigger so
i could love
you even more

hugh

# A Good Customer Base Is the Best Marketing Plan There Is

So who are your customers? Are they your marketing department? Are they actively complicit in helping your Evil Plan succeed? If they're not, they should be, yes?

**THERE'S ONE THING I REMEMBER FONDLY** about my college buddies, back in the day: Not only did they all spend a lot of time and energy listening to Grateful Dead records and attending Grateful Dead concerts, they also spent a lot of time and energy trying to get me to do the same.

Though I never became much of a hardcore Dead fan in the end (they had a couple of pretty good albums, and I'll grant that they were technically damn good musicians, but that's about it), it sure wasn't for my friends' lack of trying. My friend's powers of persuasion and peer pressure may not have worked on me, but hey, it worked on plenty of other impressionable college friends, so it's all good.

My college buddies were self-appointed team members of one of the greatest marketing departments in history: "the Deadheads"—the collective term for the Grateful Dead's massive and legendary fan base. Probably no other band in history had so many fans, spending so much time and energy trying to convert so many other people to the cause. I'm guessing a lot of them felt that the more people they could convert, the more successful the Dead would become, therefore the longer the band would be around, therefore the more concerts tickets and records in the future they'd be able to purchase. And this groove lasted for thirty years. But it was more to it than that for my college buddies. This band *mattered* to them, so it mattered to them that the Dead mattered to their friends who mattered. . . . Social and personal identity involves a lot of sharing what matters to you most, with those who matter to you most. We're primates. We're social. That's what we do.

It's an amazing thing, when your customer base not only buys your product but also consciously takes individual responsibility for your success, the way my college buddies did with the Dead. Hence my use of the term "self-appointed" earlier.

The bad news is, it's a really hard trick to pull off. The Dead managed it, so did Apple, so did the 1975 Boston Red Sox lineup, but most marketing can't achieve it even if it wants to. Your average product might be useful, offer good value, and all that market-friendly stuff, but the best Evil Plan offers something much more for people—a chance to buy into an idea that matters, and share it with people who matter to them.

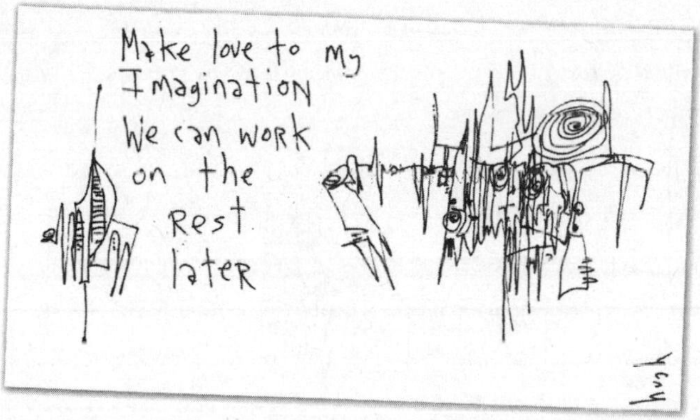
Make love to my
Imagination
We can work
on the
Rest
later

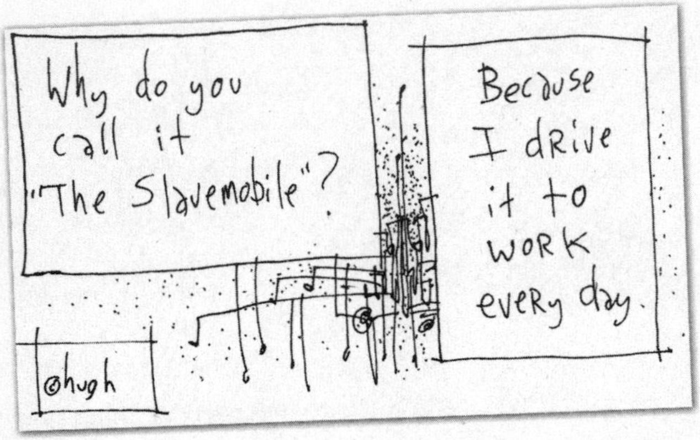
Why do you call it "The Slavemobile"?
Because I drive it to work every day.
©hugh

# Continuity Is Key

**RECENTLY I INTERVIEWED HAZEL DOONEY, A** very successful, young Australian artist. When I asked her about how she manages her business, she made a very lucid point, one that really stuck with me:

> "But none of it works without discipline. Early on in my career, I was told that success demanded one thing above all others: turning up. Turning up every bloody day, regardless of everything."

Besides reminding me of the famous Woody Allen quote "Ninety percent of success is just showing up," what Hazel said also reminds me of when I was about eighteen, living in Edinburgh. I was talking to the cartoonist Hugh Dodd, who was a regular in the bar I worked in at the time. I asked him what the secret of being a successful cartoonist was, in his opinion.

"Continuity," he said. "Anyone can draw a good cartoon . . . *once.* But not everyone can draw a good cartoon every day,

day in, day out. It's something you have to work *very hard* at for many years before you even get close. . . ."

Heh. Many years later, and I still don't feel anywhere near "close." Does anybody? But that's what keeps us marching onwards, I suppose. . . .

# Create Expressive
# Capital

Remember, we're all here to find meaning,
including your customers.

1. **First we had Human Capital.** You there! Go to the next village and kill everybody because I'm the chief of this village
   and I say so, etc.
2. **Then came Physical Capital.** Land, property, factories. "I
   give you many camels for your daughter," etc.
3. **Then came Financial Capital.** Currency, credit, stocks and
   bonds, the root of all evil, etc.
4. **Then came Intellectual Capital.** Our widgets are better
   than your widgets because our engineers are smarter than
   your engineers, etc.
5. **Then came Emotional Capital.** People love our product
   more than they love our competitor's product, etc.

So what comes after Emotional Capital? Perhaps:

6. **Expressive Capital.** Our products make it easier for the end user to find and/or express meaning, narrative, metaphor, purpose, explanation, and relevance in his/her own life than our competitor's products do.

This is why techies get so fussy about what computer they own or code they use. Or why construction workers get so into what tools they buy. It's not just about which product gets the job done, it's also about identity. Which product expresses its owner most favorably and powerfully to the world.

Not all products have Expressive Capital, of course. Most products are commodities. The trouble with commodities, of course, is that everyone's got one. And anyone who's ever dealt with Walmart or China knows what happens to those people. . . .

at the center of every human soul is the intense longing to be closer to God. an idea that can empathize with that is powerful.
hugh

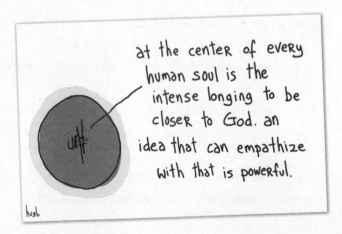

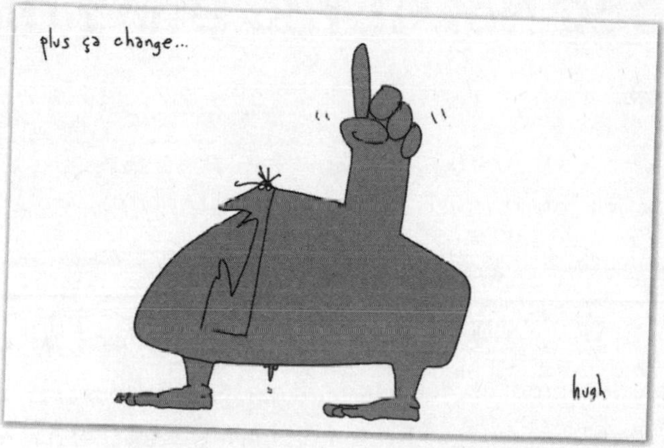
plus ça change...
hugh

# Good News! You Don't Die.

People love to imagine a worst-case scenario. Especially when it comes time to quit doing what they hate and start doing what they love instead.

**CINDI IS A VERY BRIGHT YOUNG FRIEND OF** mine with a great career in front of her. She's about twenty-six, and she's been working her tail off in New York in the graphic design industry since she graduated from college a few years ago.

Cindi grew up in a single-parent household, so there was never a lot of money around. That's OK; her mom was one smart, fun, tough cookie, and Cindi and her siblings always got good grades at school, so it all worked out rather well.

While she was getting her degree, Cindi had to pay her way through college. Happily she found this job (a) she really liked (b) was really good at, and (c) paid really good money: waiting tables at this fancy restaurant in Manhattan. She held down that job for years.

When I met her, Cindi was working for this small but kinda-sorta successful design agency, call it Acme Design (not its real name). It was founded by a pretty smart entrepreneur type, call him Joe Acme (not his real name, either).

When I met her, she was working all hours, doing a really good job. Busting ass, to put it plainly.

A few months ago, the phone rings. It's Cindi.

"I'm thinking of quitting Acme," she says.

"But I thought you really liked your job?"

"I did at first," she says. "But I don't think the company's growing anymore. Plus, I think Joe's gotten more interested in his new, far-too-young girlfriend than he is in growing the company. The same week he told us we weren't getting any new pay raises this year, he bought the chick a brand-new Audi coupe."

Ah.

"Besides," she continues, "I think I might want to start my own thing. I'm starting to get nibbles from potential clients wanting to work with me."

Ah!

"I just want to pick your brain," she says. "What do you think I ought to do?"

"Sounds like a good time to move on," I say.

"Yeah, but I'm kinda nervous about it."

"Sure, but that's normal. . . ."

So I gave her my two cents:

1. **Her mother is very supportive of her idea to move on.**
   Besides, they get on very well. So she can always move
   back home to the suburbs if she needs to save money.

2. **Acme Design is going nowhere, I can already tell.** When a
   man starts trying to shtup his way out of a midlife crisis, you
   know there's trouble afoot.

3. **Cindi tells me she has no worries about going back and
   working for the restaurant.** Not only was the money insanely
   great and she liked her job, she only quit her job at the restaurant because Joe Acme told her to.

4. **The money at Acme stinks.** Pretty much everybody who
   works there is broke by month's end. Which makes it hard
   to stand up to Joe Acme when he's having a bad day or
   having a bad idea. She was making plenty of money and
   still doing her job at Acme before Joe made her quit the
   restaurant. And since she had to give up that job, she feels
   a lot more powerless than she used to—without any increase
   in revenue. Just the opposite, in fact.

5. **Cindi doesn't mind the idea of going back to the restaurant.** I tell her to do it. At the very least, she can save some
   money that way. A young woman with an extra ten or
   twenty thousand in her pocket has a lot more room to
   maneuver than a girl who's broke at the end of every
   month.

So a simple game plan emerges: She goes and gets her old restaurant job back, she moves back in with mom to save money, she quits her job at Acme, and then she works in the mornings and afternoons for her new design clients, since her restaurant shift begins at five p.m.

When she gets off work she goes straight back home—she doesn't bother with the after-hours thing with the guys and the gals at the restaurant. No late-night booze, drugs, and club sessions for this girl. No, she's on a mission. Her colleagues at the restaurant, sadly, are not. They're too busy being young, fun, and too coked-up to tie their shoelaces, let alone do something interesting in the long-term.

She's still young. A couple more years of waiting tables won't kill her—not if she's saving money and using her off-time wisely to build her design business slowly and surely. I'd bet after a year or two, a girl with that talent and drive would easily be able to leave her waitressing job and start looking after her design clients for much better money, easily. And she'd still be well under thirty. What's the worst that can happen?

Some of Cindi's twentysomething peers raised their eyebrows a little bit, though. "Going back to waitressing? Isn't that a backwards career move?" they said.

No, it isn't, actually. She's still young and what she's doing is consistent with what she wants to do long-term. There's no disgrace in waiting tables if it's part of a long-term strategy. If she were just doing it because she had no earthly clue what else to do with her life, that would be different. But she's not.

"The good news is," I say to her, when she was just beginning to hatch this Evil Plan of hers, "you won't die."

So she went through with her Evil Plan. I was so proud. And the really good news is, she didn't have to waitress or live with her mom for very long. Three months and she was gone. Three months and she managed to bag half a dozen high-paying clients for her business. Last time I saw her, she was wearing very expensive shoes and had moved into this very hip apartment in Brooklyn. Like I said, I was so proud.

And her colleagues back at the restaurant? They're still there. Choices were made.

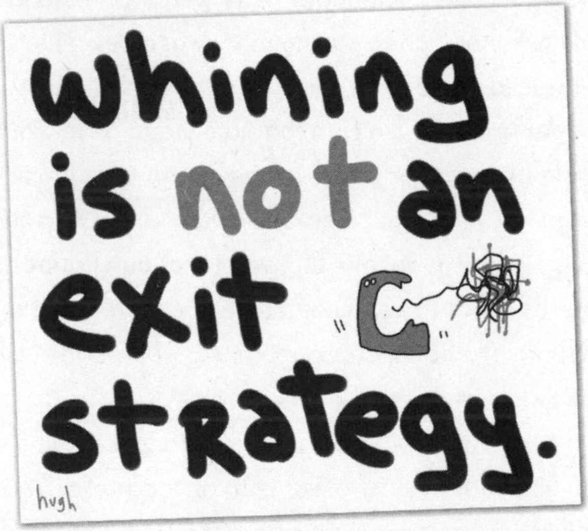
whining
is not an
exit
strategy.
hugh

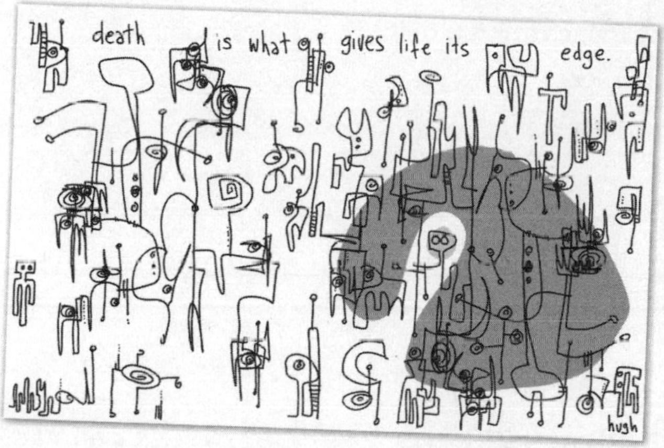
death is what gives life its edge.
hugh

# "This Is It"

It's easy to tell somebody to get into "The Zone"—
that place where work and love are unified. Much
harder to live it. But fight like hell to get there,
regardless, every friggin' day, or else you'll never
make it.

**MARK MORRIS IS A FAMOUS CONTEMPORARY**
dancer and choreographer in New York. His dance company,
the Mark Morris Dance Group tours the world, has its own
large, modern building in Brooklyn (not just the usual New York
rented loft space), and has its own school for children. He's
successful, cutting-edge, critically acclaimed and really, really
good at what he does.

I saw him being interviewed on television one evening sev-
eral years ago. He said something that really stayed with me,
something I always remember when I need a little jolt of inspi-
ration. To paraphrase:

"When new dancers come to work for my company, I tell them, *'This is it.'* In other words, this is as good as it gets. They're here to do their life's best work, or at least part of it; they're not here just to fill time and pay the bills until what they really want to do finally comes along. And I only work with dancers who can sincerely operate at that level—the people sincerely doing their life's work here and now, not dancers waiting for their lives to one day begin."

I confess, I was doing *anything but* my life's best work at the time. I was holding down a crappy, hack advertising job. Luckily times have changed since then, but at the time it was killing me, to be honest. Thank God they laid me off eventually.

We've all been there. You know you're capable of doing great things, being in "The Zone," but every external marker out there indicates otherwise—that you'll never get to do the "life's best work" that you're capable of. That your career will be nothing but drudgery and abuse in exchange for what seems an increasingly meager paycheck.

Yeah, it's a painful place to be. But it doesn't last forever, not if you don't give up. Not if you don't succumb to all the overpriced, treadmill-type external markers of success—fancy houses, cars, schools, vacations, and "stuff" that you can't really afford, that you don't really need nearly as much as the guy in the next cubicle says that you do.

This is it.

Fight like hell.

this is it.
fight like
hell.

hugh

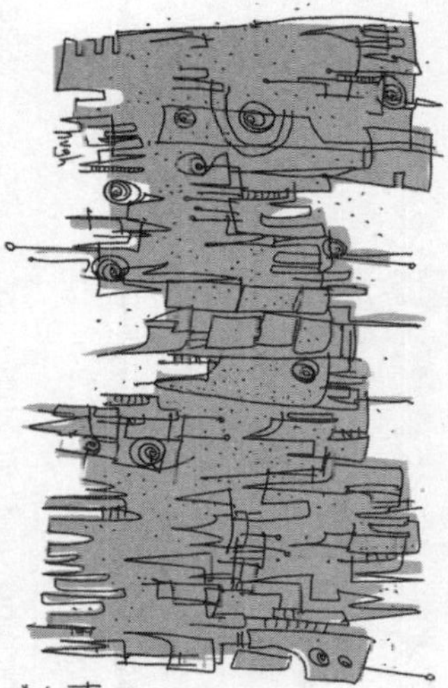
hugh

NOT DEAD. LOVED

# "Take the Cream Off the Top, Leave the Rest Behind"

**RECENTLY I WAS TALKING ON THE PHONE TO** my dear old friend Jerry Colonna, the venture-capitalist-turned-business-coach.

I was moaning and groaning about the relentless day-to-day pressure of being a small-time entrepreneur.

Jerry, in his kind, generous, lucid, and laser-focused way, reminded me that in spite of my trials and tribulations, somehow in the past year I had managed to morph from a "marketing consultant" to a full-time artist.

I guess that's exactly what has been happening. I don't quite know how I managed to pull that off—although long hours, low overhead, and a superb business partner certainly helped.

Jerry then talked about his own career evolution from successful New York venture capitalist to private business coach with a thriving practice.

Jerry told me that he simply took the cream off the part of being a VC that he liked the most—that is, helping good people make a difference—and forgot about the rest.

During this conversation, I suddenly realized that I'm now trying to do *exactly* what Jerry has already managed to do for himself: Take the cream off the top, leave the rest behind.

I can think of worse ways to spend the next couple of years. Can't you?

the
secret sauce
is:
there's no
secret sauce
hugh

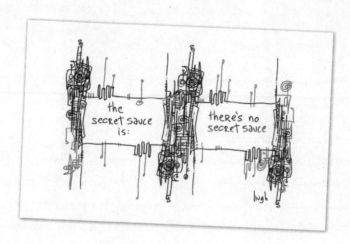

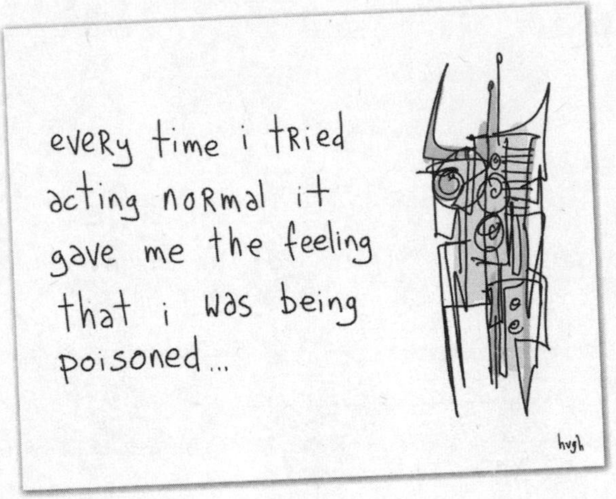

every time i tried
acting normal it
gave me the feeling
that i was being
poisoned...

hugh

# "Live in the Market, Not in the Spreadsheet"

THIS CHAPTER'S TITLE WAS COINED BY THE brilliant educator Cheryl McKinnon. Her maxim reminds me of a story.

A decade ago Howard Schultz, the founder of Starbucks, wrote a great little book about entrepreneurship, *Pour Your Heart into It: How Starbucks Built a Company One Cup at a Time.*

One story from the book that really stuck with me was about Starbucks' first *really big* crisis, sometime in the 1980s.

Basically, the international coffee market suffered a *really* bad crop that year, which drove the wholesale price sky high—enough to totally mess up the company's economic model.

Starbucks was left with one of two choices, neither of them good:

1. Start using cheaper coffee.
2. Raise prices.

Research had indicated that if they lowered the quality with cheaper coffee, only 10 percent of their customers would have palates sophisticated enough to be able to tell the difference. However if they raised their prices, *everybody* would be able to tell right away.

The accountants, predictably, recommended that they go with the cheaper coffee option. Numbers don't lie, was their reasoning; it was better to tick off 10 percent of their customers than 100 percent. Cheaper coffee was the "obvious" thing to do, they said.

Howard didn't do that in the end. Instead, he raised the prices accordingly and left a note in every store, telling people why his company was regretfully forced to raise their prices. And he also told them about the option he could've taken but chose not to .

And you know what? The customers understood his reasoning and stood by the business.

Eventually wholesale coffee prices came down again, allowing Starbucks to lower their prices as well. The company weathered the storm and the brand ended up all the stronger for it. Life was good again.

Sorry, bean counters. Numbers do lie. Sometimes pathologically . . . .

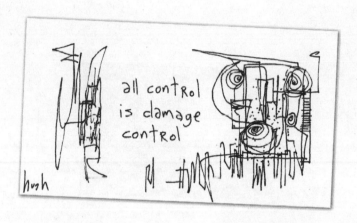

all control
is damage
control

hugh

"it is not that we have a short time to live, but that we waste a lot of it."
~ seneca
(4 b.c. - a.d. 65)

hugh

# Don't Worry If You Don't Know Absolutely Everything Before Starting Out

That's probably the last thing you need. . . .

**A LOT OF PEOPLE MASSIVELY POSTPONE THEIR** Evil Plan for the simple reason that they don't have an answer for every possible contingency.

They don't know enough about the industry. They don't know enough people in the industry—especially the A-listers. They don't know enough about where the market is going to be in five years. They don't know enough about what could possibly go wrong. They don't know where every single possible land mine is buried.

So instead of getting on with it, they spend the next few years keeping their nowheresville day job and spending their evenings surfing the Web, scouring the trade magazines, researching everything like crazy, trying to get a thorough, small-time outsider's view about what the big-time insiders are currently up to.

And then they often complicate things even further by also trying to get a handle on the even bigger stuff. For example, what will happen to the American/Asian/European/Brazilian/ Whatever economy in the next two, five, ten, twenty-five, or however many years, and how will these big things affect their tiny, obscure niche?

They want to have *all* the answers before risking getting their feet wet. Hell, before even getting one little toe wet. . . .

Agreed, a wee bit of prudence and informed circumspection are lovely virtues to have, but overdoing it can be ultimately unproductive for a variety of reasons. Here are my four favorite ones:

1. Being an outsider with too much insider knowledge makes it even more likely that you'll make the same mistakes as everybody else.

When Google—the most successful advertising business in the history of the world—started their company, their founders knew practically nothing about the inside workings of Madison Avenue. Sergey Brin and Larry Page most likely had zero inside knowledge about famous advertising titans like Leo Burnett, David Ogilvy, Lee Clowes, John Hegarty, or Claude Hopkins.

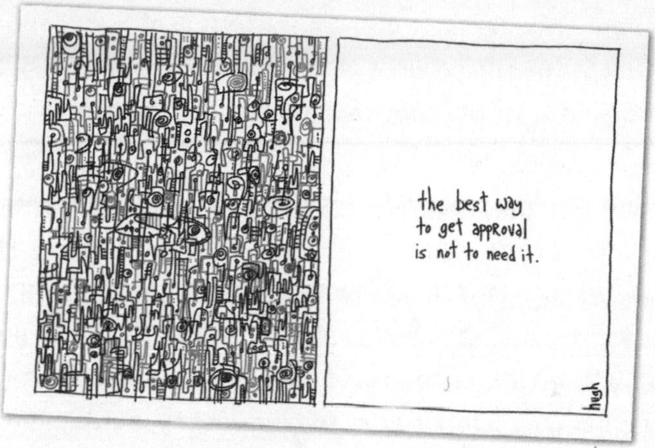
the best way
to get approval
is not to need it.
hugh

They were just a couple of twentysomething Stanford PhD students who were far more interested in Internet search engines than they ever were in Nielsen ratings, Procter & Gamble, or the Clio Awards. Which helps explain why, when the normal, mainstream, ad-industry-obsessed kids of around the same age were just landing their first East Coast internships or junior executive positions at advertising blue-chips like McCann, Lintas, DDB, or Saatchi & Saatchi, Sergey and Larry were already well on their way to becoming billionaires.

When I started my fine-art business, gapingvoidgallery.com, in late 2008, I didn't wait for the acclaim of the big-city gallery scene or a favorable review from the *New York Times* art critics before I took the plunge. First of all, those elite votes of approval were very unlikely to happen anyway, and second, even if did happen, it would have taken years and years. I just reckoned instead that (a) my blog readers already knew and liked my work, (b) a lot of them had disposable income, and (c) a lot of them had a lot of wall space that needed filling. That was all the incentive I needed to get the ball rolling.

So I just put the idea out there on my blog to see if any fish would bite. And they did. A lot of them even liked the idea enough to put up money in advance, before I had spent a single penny. As a result, the business has been profitable since day one, without me having to gain an encyclopedic knowledge of the big New York, London, and Shanghai art galleries, the current career trajectories of all the artists they represent, or the recent auction prices at Sotheby's and Christie's. Too much of that stuff would've just slowed me down, big-time.

Here are some other, far better, examples than my own: Before they launched their car companies, neither Henry Ford nor Karl Benz decided to first spend a decade trying to win the approval of prominent horse breeders or railway magnates. Same goes for the Wright Brothers.

And then there's Bill Gates. I love this story: Some years ago, when the company he founded, Microsoft, was at the height of its powers, he was giving a lecture to some college students. When the the Q&A session came along, a keen undergraduate asked the question "What advice would you give to a young person like me who wants to make a lot of money someday?"

Gates's answer was as wonderful as it was brief: "For goodness' sake, don't do what I did. That money's already been made by me."

2. "Events, dear boy, events." —Harold Macmillan, British prime minister, 1957–1963, after being asked by a young journalist what is the most likely single factor to blow any government administration off course from its long-term vision.

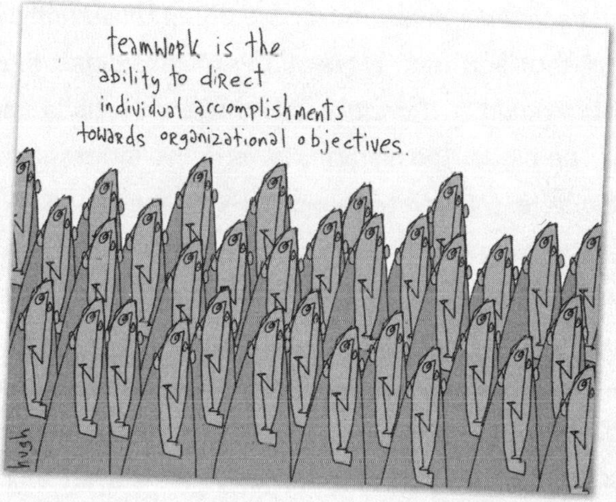
teamwork is the
ability to direct
individual accomplishments
towards organizational objectives.
hugh

If it's pretty much impossible for the smartest people in Washington, Wall Street, and Silicon Valley to predict what the big, bad world is going to do next, what chance does a guy have who wants to open a small, highly specialized, handbuilt Evil Plan bicycle operation from his small storefront in Brooklyn?

Trying to micromanage the macro-level stuff from the comfort of your wee bike shop . . . Seriously, your time is better spent trying to manage what you *can* control. Like being nice to customers; keeping your word; staying cheerful, positive, and focused; completing a task cheaper, faster, and better than you had originally promised; working harder and smarter than the next guy; fighting hard to keep your ideas fresh—in other words, all those good, small moves that Grandma told you about decades ago.

To get some very lucid, hardcore perspective on this, I recommend that you read Nassim Taleb's excellent and highly readable *Fooled by Randomness*. Taleb's thesis is childishly simple: The bigger the historical event, the more random and unpredictable the consequences. Nobody saw 9/11, Pearl Harbor, the assassinations of JFK, Julius Caesar, Lincoln, or Archduke Franz Ferdinand (and the subsequent outbreak of a four-year World War), the Atomic bombs being dropped on Japan, the 1923 collapse of the German Deutschmark, the barbarians sacking Rome in 410 A.D., the bubonic plague of the 1300s, or Hitler's 1941 invasion of the Soviet Union (and what happened afterward) coming down the pike. Ditto with Detroit not seeing the threat of Japanese cars coming after 1945 or IBM not seeing the threat posed in the 1970s by Microsoft and Apple. Everything just happened when it did, everybody was caught with their pants down, and everybody just had to deal with the massive and unpredictable consequences afterward. Not too much fun at the time, but there was no other choice. Taleb makes a damn good case.

So if your Evil Plan is to open up a two-person Internet software company, or a mom n' pop fancy cheese shop in

North Chicago, there's little point in first waiting to see if, sometime in the next two decades, whether or not India and Pakistan decide to launch nuclear missiles against each other.

3. Interesting destinies rarely come from just reading the instruction manual.

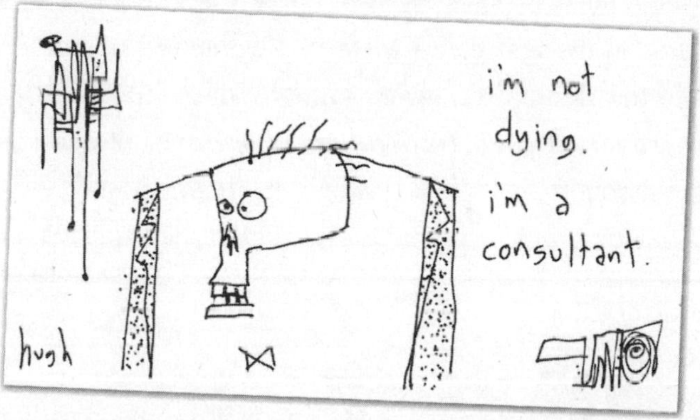
i'm not dying.
i'm a consultant.
hugh

Yes, Louis Pasteur did say "Chance favors only the prepared mind." On one level, he was right. That being said, the stuff you learn beforehand will never be one-tenth as useful as the stuff you learn the hard way, on the job. All preparation can do is help train you to deal with the reality of the actual situation. The real truth is always found in the moment, never in the future. Sadly, not everybody is cut out for thriving in the present tense. Life is unfair.

**4.** "Sometimes paranoia's just having all the facts."—attributed to William S. Burroughs

I've been in a few businesses in my time: advertising, marketing, fine-art prints, greeting cards, phone sales, animation, magazines, wine, corporate consulting, English tailoring, and now, here, book writing. Take it from me—if I had known one-half about these businesses that I know now, I doubt I would've bothered in the first place. Instead, I would've just gotten an MBA or law degree somewhere and landed a mid-level position in a bank, law firm, corporation, or whatever. Maybe joined the local country club while I was at it. Or something . . .

the world will ALWAYS conspire to make you less than you are... so decide what you're going to do about it, then act.
hugh

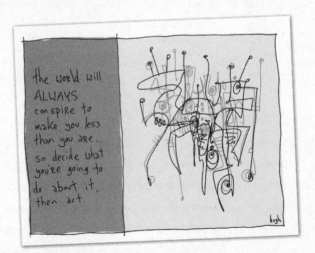

never pick a
fight with a
guy who has
nothing
to lose.

don't do
business
with him,
either...

hush

# Death by Stuff

## REMEMBER WHAT I SAID IN THE INTRODUCTION:

## "TO UNIFY WORK AND LOVE"

Sigmund Freud once said that in order to be truly happy in life, a human being needed to acquire two things: the capacity to work, and the capacity to love.

An Evil Plan is really about being able to do both at the same time.

So how do you do both at the same time?

Easy: You love what you do.

How do you love what you do?

You make the decision to do so.

The earlier in your life you make that decision, the easier your Evil Plan will be to pull off.

The easier it will be to actually create something.

The longer you've been working, the more you see this: people in their thirties and forties who have kind of hit the wall in their career trajectory but somehow need the money more than ever.

You know, to pay for all that "stuff." Fancy cars, nice houses in the suburbs, golf clubs, that kinda thing.

They hate their work, but they love their "stuff."

They say they have no choice. They have children, mortgages, responsibilities, that sort of thing.

But they also have a lot of "stuff," which requires ever more time and money to enjoy properly, to keep the veneer from cracking.

Because the older you get, the more time and energy is needed to compensate for the fact that basically, you hate what you do. That you've never liked what you do. That all along, it's always been about the "stuff."

Those people always get crucified, eventually. Their bosses always get rid of them, eventually.

So please decide to love what you do—the sooner, the better. "Death by Stuff" is really no way to live.

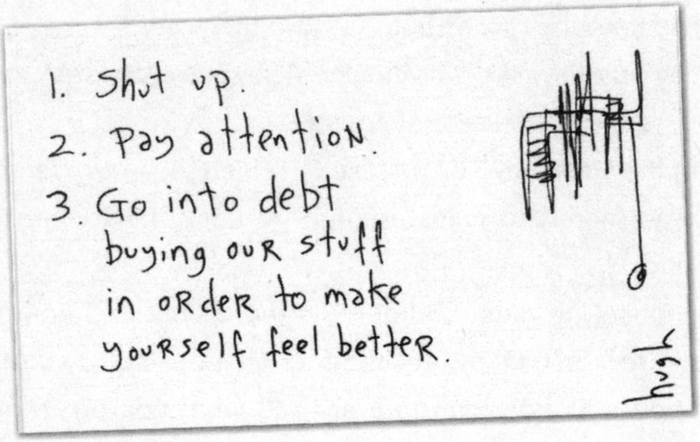

1. Shut up.
2. Pay attention.
3. Go into debt
   buying our stuff
   in order to make
   yourself feel better.

hugh

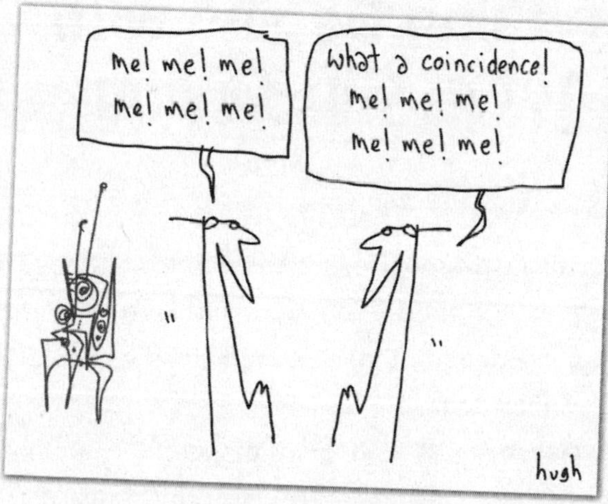
me! me! me!
me! me! me!
what a coincidence!
me! me! me!
me! me! me!
hugh

# Everything Begins with the Act of Gift-Giving

**BRIAN CLARK DOES IT. GARY VAYNERCHUK** does it. James Governor does it. Dennis Howlett does it. John T. Unger does it. Robert Scoble does it. Fred Wilson does it. Jerry Colonna does it. Esther Dyson does it. Sonia Simone does it. A.V. Flox does it.

These eleven smart, kind, great bloggers—some more well-known than others—are masters at what I call "Selling by Giving."

They put stuff out there as gifts. Great content, great ideas, great insights, great personal connection. By giving so much of themselves, for free, every day, they build up huge surpluses of goodwill, so when you're finally in the market for something they're selling (and they're *all* selling something, trust me), they're first on your list.

I try to follow their example. Every weekday morning I send out a new cartoon to my e-mail list (gapingvoid.com/n2). We're talking many, many thousands of people.

It's my daily "gift" to the world, as it were. . . .

One gift per day, that's my quota. Anything more and I get too swamped. I also work hard to make sure that it feels like a gift on the receiving end. I try to put some heart and soul into the exercise; otherwise, people would unsubscribe in droves.

If enough people like the gift, it'll build up goodwill, they'll tell their friends, and the list grows. The more the list grows, the more people discover the trail of breadcrumbs that leads back to the work I actually get paid for—fine-art prints and commission work. I put a few links in there to my paid work, but nothing too obtrusive. No conventional sales message to speak of. I feel that if people are in the market for what I make, they're smart people; they'll click on the links eventually.

And even if people don't follow the breadcrumbs, the vast majority of the time, that's OK too. I'm happy if people just dig my work and value the gift. Not everybody's in the market for my paid work—I'm not in the market for everything my friends do either. That doesn't mean I don't value them or their gifts highly. It cuts both ways.

It can't be selfish. You can't expect something back in return. It can't be hucksterish. People can tell, you see. . . .

Everything I do now professionally begins with the act of gift-giving. What about you?

1. Figure out what your gift is, and give it to people on a regular basis.

2. Make sure it's received as a real gift, not as an advertising message.
3. Then figure out exactly what it is that your trail of breadcrumbs leads back to.

Just do these three things, and all your marketing dreams will come true, I promise.

communing
with the
divine.
©hugh

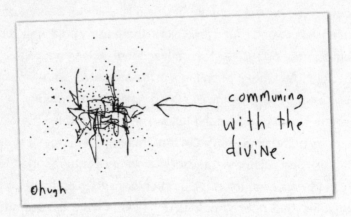

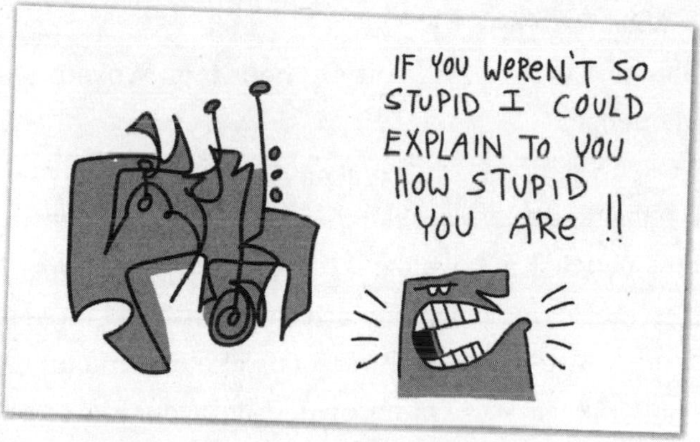
IF YOU WEREN'T SO STUPID I COULD EXPLAIN TO YOU HOW STUPID YOU ARE !!

# Be a Waker

## ARE YOU A "WAKER"?

If the answer is no, I'm sorry to hear that. Wakers are my favorite people.

A waker is someone who is very good at waking other people up from their metaphorical slumber, temporary or otherwise.

Some people just have the gift. Being around them or their work just makes you feel more alive, more inspired, more motivated, more *awake*. The best wakers will make you do crazy-ass things, like quit your boring job and start your own business, write that song, move to Thailand, forgive that someone who once hurt you, or finally tell that girl that you love her.

A waker reminds you on a constant basis *just how alive you really are*. Just how much human potential you really have inside of you. And there's something about their influence that makes you utterly unable to go back to "sleep" ever again, despite your best efforts.

Wakers can be great artists—Jeff Buckley, Picasso, Harper Lee, Beethoven, Judy Garland, Charlie Parker, Leo Tolstoy, Louis Armstrong, Ralph Steadman, Dorothy Parker, etc.—but they don't have to be.

Wakers can be great spiritual leaders—Jesus, Gandhi, Mohammed, Buddha, the Dalai Lama, Mother Teresa, Martin Luther King, Joseph Campbell, etc.—but they don't have to be.

Wakers can be great public figures—Steve Jobs, Winston Churchill, Mike Royko, Oprah Winfrey, Carl Sagan, John Peel, Susan Sontag, Alistair Cooke, Margaret Thatcher, Bill Murray, etc.—but they don't have to be.

I know great wakers who are bartenders, bus drivers, waitresses, teachers, receptionists, plumbers. Theirs is a gift, not a job title.

If you are a waker, I'm happy for you. There is no better way to spend one's life than being a waker; I truly believe that.

The human race needs you, like flowers need sunshine. The human race would die out within three generations without you. Thanks for being here. Seriously.

If you're not a waker, don't you think you should be? Serious question.

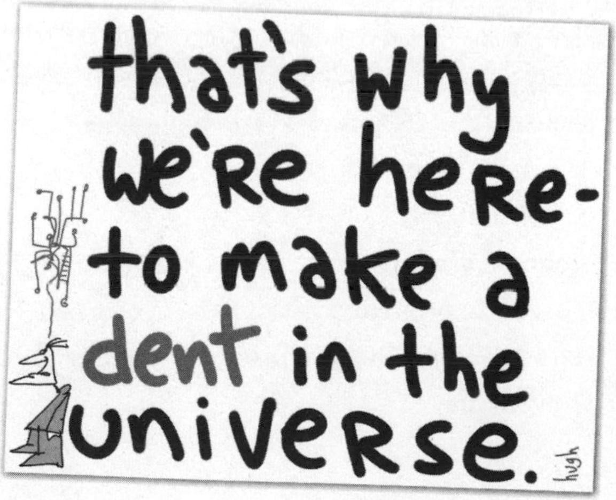
that's why we're here- to make a dent in the universe.
hugh

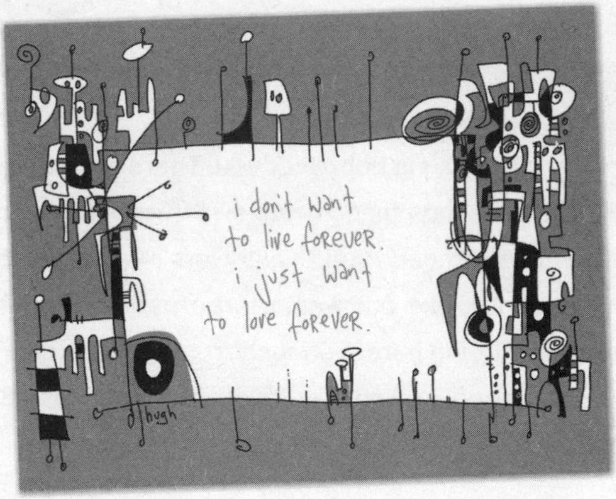
i don't want
to live forever.
i just want
to love forever.
hugh

# Human Beings Don't Scale

**LARRY ELLISON, THE CEO OF ORACLE, MAY** have a million times more money than me, but he isn't going to live a million times longer than me, watch a million times more sunsets than me, make love to a million times more women than me, drink a million times more fine wines than me, listen to a million times more Beethoven string quartets than me, or have a million times more grandchildren than me. Human beings don't scale.

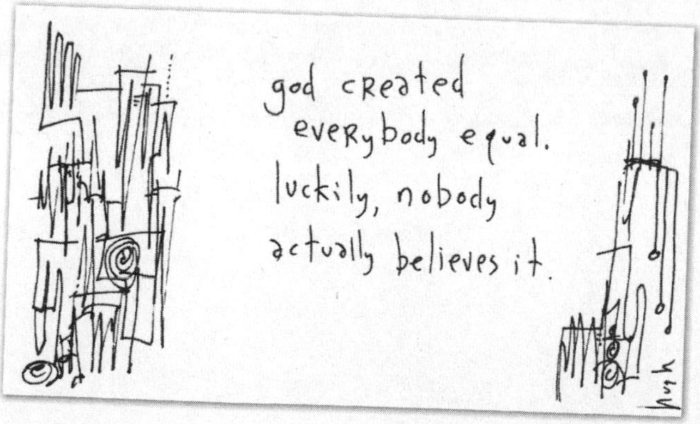
god created
everybody equal.
luckily, nobody
actually believes it.
hugh

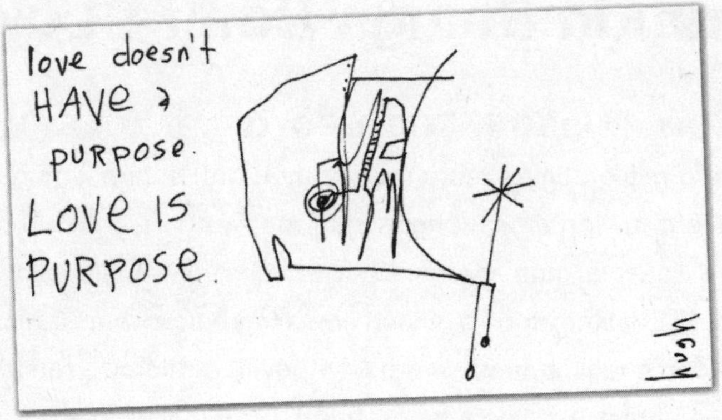
love doesn't
HAVE a
purpose.
LOVE IS
PURPOSE.

# Evil Plans Are Not Products; Evil Plans Are Gifts

You were given a gift by the Creator, God, the Universe . . . Whatever. Until you have returned the favor, life will have a certain, feckless emptiness to it.

**SO, SOONER OR LATER YOU'RE GOING TO HAVE** to explain to your friends and family *exactly* why you decided to quit your stable 401(k) job and go off on some long-term act of *lunacy*—by which I mean your Evil Plan.

I don't know what exactly you'll tell them. I do know, however, that somewhere in the back of your mind will be a feeling that you have something you want to give to the world, something that you haven't given yet, something the world needs but doesn't yet quite know it.

Yes, you have already learned how to make a living and pay the bills. . . .

But you know that's not enough.

I've had my fair share of crappy jobs, as have we all. You know what? I never hated a job because of what it took from me—*all* jobs take a lot from you, especially the best ones.

I hated a job because it never allowed me to *give* enough to the world.

That's all I ever wanted: my best self, playing my best game. Being an advertising hack never allowed that, somehow. It never allowed me to fully give what I thought I was capable of. But I can now do that as a cartoonist.

I'm damn lucky to have found that out, even if it did take me a painfully, embarrassingly long time.

I'm not the world's most talented person at what I do. Neither are you. That doesn't make the gifts we have any less valid.

Giving the gift is an act of love. And love is the only thing that matters.

That's why we have an Evil Plan. Because it matters. Because love matters.

What else is there to say? . . .

# Your Evil Pl

Get out there and get you

Feel free to use the

scribble down some of th

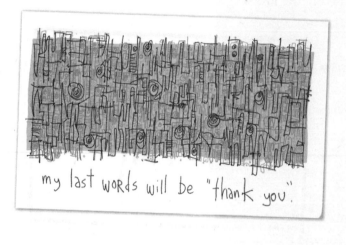

my last words will be "thank you".

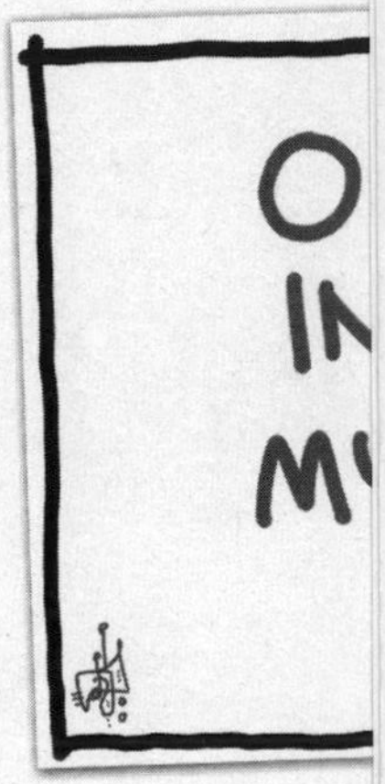

O
IN
M